Creation Sings Your Praise

Annabel Shilson-Thomas is an Anglican priest in Cambridge, where she is Associate Vicar of Great St Mary's, the University Church, and Chaplain to Michaelhome. She was previously the spirituality Writer and consultant for the development agency CAFOD, and edited *Livesimply – A CAFOD resource for living simply, sustainably and in solidarity.*

Christian Aid is a Christian organization that insists the world can and must be swiftly changed to one where everyone can lead a full life, free from poverty. It works globally for profound change that eradicates the causes of poverty, striving to achieve equality, dignity and freedom for all, regardless of faith or nationality. It is part of a wider movement for social justice. It provides urgent, practical and effective assistance where need is great, tackling the effects of poverty as well as its roots.

Titles published with Christian Aid from Canterbury Press

The Christian Aid Book of Bread: Recipes to Change Your World
Sarah Stancliffe   978 1 85311 626 1

**The Christian Aid Book of Simple Feasts: Cooking for a Crowd
through the Christian Year**
Sarah Stancliffe   978 1 85311 836 X

**Harvest for the World: A Worship Anthology on Sharing in the
Work of Creation**
Edited by Geoffrey Duncan   978 1 85311 574 5

Let Justice Roll Down: A Christian Aid/CAFOD Resource for Lent
Edited by Geoffrey Duncan   978 1 85311 555 4

**Shine On, Star of Bethleham: A Worship Anthology for Advent,
Christmas and Epiphany**
Edited by Geoffrey Duncan   978 1 85311 588 2

www.canterburypress.co.uk

Creation Sings Your Praise

A Christian Aid Worship Book

Edited by

Annabel Shilson-Thomas

© In this compilation Christian Aid 2010

First published in 2010 by the Canterbury Press Norwich
Editorial office
13–17 Long Lane,
London, EC1A 9PN, UK

Canterbury Press is an imprint of Hymns Ancient and Modern Ltd
(a registered charity)
13A Hellesdon Park Road,
Norwich, NR6 5DR, UK

www.scm-canterburypress.co.uk

British Library Cataloguing in Publication data

A catalogue record for this book is available
from the British Library

978 1 85311 890 6

Typeset by Regent Typesetting, London
Printed and bound in Great Britain by
CPI William Clowes, Beccles NR34 7TL

Contents

Acknowledgements

As always, the real debt of thanks goes to all those extraordinary people who live lives of ingenuity, daily surviving against the odds and so demonstrating that each day is a gift. They are the inspiration behind the pages in this book.

Many of the liturgies and prayers have grown out of Christian Aid's work among such people, while others come from partner organizations, in particular from Christian Aid's partners in South Africa who have contributed generously to the contents of this book.

From conception to delivery, Christine Smith at Canterbury Press and Kate Tuckett at Christian Aid, have encouraged this project, waiting patiently for the book to come to birth, while at home, my husband Hugh has long been in sympathetic labour, generously supported by our children Aidan and Freya. To them I owe grateful thanks, as I do, to my colleague John Binns at Great St Mary's for providing the space to shut myself away when needed.

Foreword

The rhythms of the Christian year give us a framework within which we can enter more deeply into the life and love of God. As we live and pray through Advent waiting and Christmas incarnation; the ashes of Lent, temptation, betrayal and suffering; the joy of Easter through to the coming of the Spirit; and then the observation of the ministry of Jesus until the end of the year when we look forward till the end of time, we are drawn into a living relationship with the God of love that we worship.

This God of unity, this Trinity of love, invites us into a spirituality of encounter. As we live out Jesus' life and ministry in our worship, we can be inspired by his relentless pushing at all the divisions that separate, and his insistence that to be truly and fully human is to belong together. We believe that as we are all invited into a relationship with a God of love and community, our relationships with one another must show the same characteristics of love and justice that God shows to us. When relationships are broken, our development work demands that we restore them if our relationship with God is not to be flawed.

It is our hope that this collection of liturgies and prayers will help you to explore in worship how God calls us to live in relationship in an unjust world. At Christian Aid we believe that poverty can be ended and the world can be changed. And we believe that if, as the Bible tells us, human beings are made in God's image, we can strive for nothing less. It is our vocation, our calling.

History has shown us that remarkable change can happen very quickly. The defeat of apartheid and the eradication of smallpox, for example, both took place within a decade. And the world can change very quickly. The Haiti earthquake, which happened as the manuscript for this book was being completed, is one example of how suddenly and unexpectedly disaster can strike. But there is always hope. The huge generosity of the public in response to this disaster, as well as the inspirational work of Christian Aid partners in rebuilding and reconstruction are powerful testimony to the hope that can emerge when we work together for change. The Christian Aid website contains information about and prayers for the most up-to-the-minute news and campaigns. We encourage you to visit it at www.christianaid.org.uk when planning your worship.

We owe a particular debt of thanks to the South African partners who have generously contributed material to this volume. Standing alongside them in our prayer and worship is one expression of our unity and solidarity for justice. Christian Aid's work is all about empowering people and communities to lead a full life in all its aspects. But standing in unity is deeply transformative for our worship communities here. It is our prayer that this resource will go some way to empowering your church community to stand in unity with those all over the world who are working for peace, justice and reconciliation, and to be changed in the process.

Loretta Minghella
Director, Christian Aid

Preface

Creation Sings Your Praise is a joyful title. Often, though, the proclamation of God's justice, which is what this book celebrates, is equated with sombre pronouncements of human failings rather than the abundant generosity of God. It would seem that it is easier to focus on the injustice of poverty, highlighting the disparity between those who have too much and those who have too little, rather than to look at the poverty of our relationships which is where injustice begins.

When we lose sight of our maker, in whose image we are made, we lose sight of our responsibility to each other and our connectedness with the earth. Rather than hearing creation sing the praises of the Creator we are seduced by the sound of our own voices proclaiming the power of the creature. We become deaf to the 'heavens declaring God's glory and the firmament his handiwork' and mute in our own declaration of praise; for with praise comes recognition of our place within creation and of our call to care for the earth and one another.

But God's grace abounds and his generosity is never spent. Just as the Prodigal Son is met by the open arms of his father, when we turn to God we are welcomed home – home to a place both of acceptance and challenge, nurture and growth. Without these four things, we become inert in the face of injustice, being weighed down by our own guilt and the enormity of the task ahead. It is hoped that, in some small way, the liturgies, prayers and reflections in this book may offer a way into accepting the place from where we start and provide the challenge to see things afresh, while nurturing seeds of transformation and inspiring the kind of growth that leads to change.

Much of this material has grown out of reflection on the struggles of communities and churches, at home and overseas, as we try to make sense of the world we know and seek to respond to its needs in a way that is life-giving. As always, life is never static and situations change so the focus of Christian Aid's work is constantly under review, as its up-to-the minute website reflects. But some things remain constant – our interconnectedness as human beings and the mutuality of our need to engage with one another. Shortly after this manuscript was completed, the Haiti earthquake struck, metaphorically shaking the world as its devastating effects became clear and our lack of control over nature was spelt out. What also became evident was the power of solidarity, when communities – otherwise separated by every conceivable barrier, land, sea, language and culture – are bound together by a common humanity and the desire to ensure that death does not have the last word. Ultimately, this is what this book and Christian Aid proclaims; that there is life before death and that it is a life to be lived and celebrated within the song of creation.

Annabel Shilson-Thomas
Easter 2010

Part One

Seasonal Liturgies

Advent, Christmas and Epiphany

Advent

Advent marks the beginning of the Church's year when Christians look forward to the birth of the Christ-child. It is a time of watching and waiting, of eager expectation and longing for all that is to come. And as we wait in the metaphorical darkness, hoping and praying for the fulfilment of God's promise, we are minded to search ourselves in readiness for the dawning light, reflecting on all that separates us from God and preparing to meet him in his son, Jesus Christ.

LOOKING BACKWARDS AND FORWARDS

Preparation

You will need an Advent wreath with four outer candles and one central candle, and hand-held candles for everyone present.

Welcome and call to worship

Leader	In this season of Advent, let us give thanks for the past year, for work done and changes made; and as we look forward in joyful anticipation to the birth of the Christ-child, let us commit ourselves to a new vision of a just world.
Leader	In our watching and our waiting,
All	**come, Lord Jesus.**
Leader	In our hopes and in our fears,
All	**come, Lord Jesus.**

Leader	In our homes and in our world,
All	**come, Lord Jesus.**

Leader	Come, Lord Jesus, bless and surprise us,
	as we look forward to your birth day.
All	**Amen.**

Hymn

Looking back over the last year

Individuals and groups are invited to offer their reflections on the previous year, in whatever media they prefer, highlighting challenges, changes and transformations.

Song of thanksgiving

Reading A voice cries out: 'In the wilderness prepare the way of the LORD, make straight in the desert a highway for our God. Every valley shall be lifted up, and every mountain and hill be made low; the uneven ground shall become level, and the rough places a plain. Then the glory of the LORD shall be revealed, and all people shall see it together, for the mouth of the LORD has spoken. A voice says, 'Cry out!' And I said, 'What shall I cry?' All people are grass, their constancy is like the flower of the field. The grass withers, the flower fades, when the breath of the LORD blows upon it; surely the people are grass. The grass withers, the flower fades; but the word of our God will stand forever.

Isaiah 40.3–8

Lighting of the Advent wreath

As each of the four outer candles is lit, thanks are offered for something specific over the previous year.

Lighting of the central candle and prayer of commitment

Leader	Let us give thanks for all who work towards a more just society, and for all that has been achieved so far, and let us renew our vision of a transformed world, asking God to light our way forward.

All God of power, God of people,
    you are the life of all that lives,
    the energy that fills the earth,
    the vitality that brings to birth,
    the impetus toward making whole
    whatever is bruised or broken.

    You are the song the whole earth sings,
    the promise that liberation brings.
    You are the truth
    that sets us free.
    To you we commit ourselves anew
    with Advent hope to guide us through.

Looking forward

Lighting of the candles of promise and procession

Everyone is offered a candle to be lit as a symbol of God's promise of light in the darkness and their commitment to follow the light. When the candles are lit, everyone processes to the door while singing 'We are marching in the light of God'. Before exiting, the blessing is given.

Blessing

Leader May the God of the poor challenge us to work for justice.
    May Christ our deliverer give us hope for the future.
    May the Spirit of truth shine in our darkness and bring us
     peace.
    And may the blessing of God,
    Creator, Redeemer and Sustainer,
    be with us all, now and for evermore.
    Amen.

PREPARING THE WAY OF THE LORD: JUGGLING OUR PRIORITIES

Introduction and welcome

As people enter, music is played, while a juggler juggles. When everyone is seated, the music draws to a close and the first reading is read while the juggler juggles faster and faster until all the balls are dropped.

Readings

Reader 1 John the Baptist went into all the regions around the Jordan, proclaiming a baptism of repentance for the forgiveness of sins, as it is written in the book of the words of the prophet Isaiah:

> 'The voice of one crying out
>   in the wilderness:
> Prepare the way of the Lord,
>   Make his paths straight . . .'

Luke 3.3–4

Reader 2 Alice could never quite make out, thinking about it afterwards, how it was that they began. All she remembers is that they were running hand in hand, and the Queen went so fast that it was all she could do to keep up with her. The Queen kept crying, 'Faster, faster!' but Alice felt she could not go faster. The most curious part was that the trees round them never changed their places at all. However fast they went, they never seemed to pass anything. Then Alice looked around with great surprise. 'Why, I do believe we've been under this tree the whole time. Everything's just as it was.'

'Of course,' said the Queen. 'How else would you have it?'

'Well, in our country,' said Alice, panting a little, 'you would generally get to somewhere else if you ran fast for a long time.'

'A slow sort of country,' said the Queen. 'Here it takes all the running you can do to keep in the same place. If you want to get somewhere else, you must run at least twice as fast as that!'

From Alice Through the Looking Glass *by Lewis Carroll*

Leader Welcome to our worship. During this service we will think about how we prepare to meet God amongst the competing demands of our lives. How do we juggle the competing priorities in our lives – work, home, prayer and neighbour? We will think about what 'Preparing the way of the Lord', the great Advent theme, is about – is it about doing more and more or about being open to receive God's light so we can find the right path along which to journey?

6

The first reading we heard was from the opening chapters of Luke's Gospel when John the Baptist prepares the way for Jesus' ministry. The second was from *Alice Through the Looking Glass*; and the third is from St Anselm, who was Archbishop of Canterbury in the 11th century.

Reader 3   Come now, little one, turn aside for a while. Enter the inner chamber of your soul. Shut out everything except God. Now, my whole heart, say to God, 'I seek your face; Lord, it is your face I seek.'

St Anselm

There follows a short period of silence for quiet reflection.

Seeking God's face

Psalm

Leader	My heart says of God, 'Seek his face!'
All	**Your face, Lord, I will seek.**
Leader	The Lord is my light and my salvation.
All	**Therefore whom shall I fear?**
Leader	The Lord is the stronghold of my life.
All	**Of whom shall I be afraid?**
Leader	Teach me your way, O Lord.
All	**Lead me to walk in a straight path.**
Leader	Though an army besiege me,
All	**My heart will not know panic.**
Leader	Though war break out all around me.
All	**Even then will I be confident.**
Leader	Hear my voice when I call, O Lord.
All	**In my confusion, be merciful to me and answer me.**
Leader	Wait for the Lord.
All	**Be strong and take heart and wait for the Lord.**
Leader	For in the day of many troubles he will keep me safe in his dwelling.
All	**He will hide me in his shelter and set me upon a rock.**
Leader	My heart says of God, 'Seek his face!'
All	**Your face, Lord, I will seek.**

From Psalm 27

Reflection based on Ephesians 5.8–21

Leader How can we manage better the constant demands on our time that 21st-century living seems to involve, so that our focus is ultimately on God, not on keeping all the balls in the air?

    If we were to go on a time-management course, we would be invited to focus on four things to help us prioritize and order our lives better.

1 Clarification of our personal goals.
2 Our use of time.
3 Valuable habits and skills.
4 Our skills with people.

    Curiously, these four things are precisely what Paul impressed upon the church at Ephesus. So let us look at what Paul said in his letter to the Ephesians which today's Time Managers recognize as relevant.

    Let's start with the clarification of personal goals.

Reader 3 Paul wrote: 'You were once darkness, but now you are light in the Lord. Live as children of light, that is, seek out goodness, righteousness and truth, and make a priority of finding out what pleases the Lord.'

Leader What would you like to do that reflects God's light? Now, before Christmas, in the next year, in the future? And how do you think these things will please the Lord?

Silence

Leader Now let's look at how we use our time.

Reader 3 Paul wrote: 'Be very careful, then, how you live – not as unwise but as wise, making the most of every opportunity, because the days are evil. Understand what the Lord's will is.'

Leader What things do you do that waste more time than they achieve? What would it take for you to stop? Is this realistic? With what would you fill the space that you gain?

Silence

Leader   Next, let's look at developing valuable habits and skills.

Reader 3   Paul wrote: 'Do not get drunk on wine. Instead, be filled with the Spirit. Sing and make music in your heart to the Lord, always giving thanks to God the Father for everything, in the name of our Lord Jesus Christ.'

Leader   Hmm! Only you will know whether the habits and skills that Paul talks about are ones that would help you. But if they aren't, what are?

Silence

Leader   Finally, let's think about our people skills.

Reader 3   Paul wrote: 'Submit to one another out of reverence for Christ.'

Leader   Sometimes that will mean being available to people when it doesn't entirely suit us. And saying 'yes' to calls on our time will also mean learning to say 'no' to other calls on our time. Again, it is a question of what we prioritize: what we take up and what we give up; and can we do both sensitively in a way that reverences Christ.

Silence

'Pax', a poem by D. H. Lawrence

Reader 1   All that matters is to be at one with the living God
to be a creature in the house of the God of Life.

Like a cat asleep on a chair
at peace, in peace
and at one with the master of the house, with the mistress,
at home, at home in the house of the living,
sleeping on the hearth, and yawning before the fire.

Sleeping on the hearth of the living world,
yawning at home before the fire of life
feeling the presence of the living God
like a great reassurance
a deep calm in the heart
a presence

as of a master sitting at the board
in his own and greater being,
in the house of life.

Song   'Be still for the presence of the Lord' (or another meditative song)

Prayer

Leader   And so we commit our thoughts to God using the words of
          Psalm 37:
          Trust in the Lord and do good;
All   **dwell in the land and enjoy safe pasture.**
Leader   Delight yourself in the Lord;
All   **and he will give you the desires of your heart.**
Leader   Commit your way to the Lord;
All   **trust in him and this is what he will do:**
Leader   He will make your righteousness shine like the dawn,
All   **works of justice like the noonday sun.**
Leader   Be still before the Lord and wait patiently;
All   **do not fret and refrain from anger.**
Leader   A little while, and the wicked will be no more;
All   **but the meek of the land will enjoy great peace.**

Blessing

Leader   Let us join together in the words of blessing from Arch-
          bishop Helder Camera of Brazil, and let us go out into the
          world to prepare the way of the Lord by opening our hearts
          to his promptings.
All   **Go down**
          into the plans of God.
          Go down
          deep as you may.
          Fear not
          for your fragility
          under that weight of water.
          Fear not
          for life or limb
          sharks attack savagely.
          Fear not the power

of treacherous currents under the sea.
Simply, do not be afraid.
Let go. You will be led
like a child whose mother
holds him to her bosom
and against all comers is his shelter.

FROM DARKNESS TO LIGHT: A SERVICE FOR WORLD AIDS DAY

Many people have come to associate the beginning of Advent with World AIDS Day, which falls on 1 December. The occasion provides an opportunity both for repentance and renewal, two of the great Advent themes; repentance for the prejudice surrounding the treatment of those affected by HIV, and renewal of our commitment to fight the stigma endured by many living with HIV.

Preparation

Position a large candle in a central position.

Introduction

Opening responses

Leader	A new day has dawned.
	Hope greets us anew.
All	**Thanks be to God.**
Leader	Let us then bring our greetings to God.
All	**God we have come to greet you this morning.**
Leader	We are your world and your people.
All	**You created us with your hands.**
Leader	We are made in your likeness.
All	**You created us in your image.**
Leader	We are people of your love.
All	**You created us and you created us good.**
Leader	O God, you are the source of our life.
	Gather us now, together, we pray.

11

Form us into a holy community of your own people.
Mould us by the breath of your Holy Spirit and
reveal in the corporate body
the face of your anointed Christ. Amen.

Lighting a candle of hope

Leader   As we become increasingly conscious of God's presence with
us, let us light our candle of hope.

The candle is lit.

Leader   The lighting of this candle reminds us that there is a light
that shines in the darkness and the darkness has not overcome it. It is lit for any within our communities living with
HIV and for the 33 million people living with HIV around
the world. Ninety-six per cent of these people live in developing countries.
          The flame is both a symbol of the embracing warmth of
the light that shines within the darkness of our shared pain
and a symbol of the hope that is hidden in the mystery of our
lives, and of the lives of those whom we remember today.

So let us worship our Lord:
the Lord who touched the lepers,
the Lord who touched the lonely,
the Lord who waits to touch our hearts today.

We pray together:

All   **Lord Jesus, you are our light that shines in the darkness.
We light this candle to remind ourselves that we can find
your light at the centre of our lives. So wonderful is your
light that it dispels the darkness of even the darkest night
and leads us to the glory of the morning and a new day.**

Hymn   'Lord, the light of your love is shining' (or another suitable
hymn)

Opening our hearts

Leader   Let us pray:

God of all humanity,
in a world full of fear,
open our hearts to your love,
our minds to your hope
and our eyes to your light.
Turn us from hatred towards love,
from intolerance towards understanding,
from judgement to compassion
that together we may pray for wholeness
and, as sisters and brothers, work for peace. Amen.

Reading   Do not judge, so that you may not be judged. For with the
judgement you make you will be judged, and the measure
you give will be the measure you get.

Matthew 7.1–2

Hymn   'Be still and know that I am God' (or another suitable
hymn)

Meditation

Reading

Reader   Just then a lawyer stood up to test Jesus. Teacher,' he said,
'what must I do to inherit eternal life?' He said to him,
'What is written in the law? What do you read there?' He
answered, 'You shall love the Lord your God with all your
heart, and with all your soul, and with all your strength, and
with all your mind; and your neighbour as yourself.' And he
said to him, 'You have given the right answer; do this, and
you will live.' But wanting to justify himself, he asked Jesus,
'And who is my neighbour?'

   Jesus replied, 'A man was going down from Jerusalem
to Jericho, and fell into the hands of robbers, who stripped
him, beat him, and went away, leaving him half dead. Now
by chance a priest was going down that road; and when he
saw him, he passed by on the other side. So likewise a Levite,
when he came to the place and saw him, passed by on the
other side. But a Samaritan while travelling came near him;
and when he saw him, he was moved with pity. He went to
him and bandaged his wounds, having poured oil and wine

on them. Then he put him on his own animal, brought him to an inn, and took care of him. The next day he took out two denarii, gave them to the innkeeper, and said, "Take care of him; and when I come back, I will repay you whatever more you spend." Which of these three, do you think, was a neighbour to the man who fell into the hands of the robbers?' He said, 'The one who showed him mercy.' Jesus said to him, 'Go and do likewise.'

Luke 10.25–37

Leader   The parable of the Good Samaritan is one of the most well known in the Bible, and its familiarity can mask the uncomfortable truth at its centre.

It is not just a story about helping people in need. The Samaritans were a marginalized people; they were despised by the Jews, who were the primary audience for the story. The priest and the Levite, on the other hand, would both have enjoyed status and respect among the Jews. Yet it is the Samaritan – not the priest or the Levite – who stops to help the injured traveller.

Indeed, the story is a radical call to action. It is about helping our immediate neighbours, and about crossing religious and cultural barriers. We must take inspiration from the Samaritan and reach out across barriers to help people living with HIV – both on the other side of the world and closer to home.

The Samaritan asks no questions. We do not know why the traveller is there, or how he has suffered his injuries. Such details are irrelevant; all we know is that he needs love and care. The Samaritan's goodness is in being there and being prepared to get involved in a situation which he probably felt inadequate to handle. The marginalized Samaritan is held up as the moral example. If the priest had attended to the traveller's needs, his actions would have made him impure and he would have been unable to offer prayers and sacrifices. As a church, are we overly concerned with being respectable? Do we place too much importance on religious expectation? Or are we ready to reach out to those who need us most?

Christian Aid supports the world of Inerela+, an international network of religious leaders living with HIV, which provides peer education programmes in 40 of the world's poorest countries. It also promotes the voices of people living with HIV as key partners in its programmes. Christian Aid's work has shown that it is often those people who, like the Samaritan, are in situations that place them as 'outsiders' who can provide the most effective healing and comfort.

We might ask ourselves whether we, as a church, give opportunities to marginalized people and groups within our own communities. Do we offer their potential in offering support and comfort to others? Do we concern ourselves with reconciliation for those who are alienated from society – through sickness, gender, race, colour, or any other means?

The warning in the parable is clear – it is easy to make an excuse to do nothing; it is easy to walk by on the other side of the road, to tell ourselves that we have more important matters to attend. But with around 5,700 people dying every single day from HIV-related illnesses, we cannot afford to walk on by. Jesus makes it clear that if we are to follow his way, we must follow the path of the Samaritan.

Prayers

Leader   Let us pray:

Good teacher, you were accused.
You offended common decency
by touching people labelled as 'unclean'.
Like the 'righteous', we want you to bless us, not them –
not the marginalized and misunderstood:
the Samaritans, lepers, tax collectors, women and children.
We want you to confirm our prejudices
but you shatter them and touch those we shun.
We're not sure we can follow you in this way
for we fear those you bless.
We are closed to the depth and breadth of your grace.
Forgive us, Father.
Turn our fear into acts of courage,
our condemnation into compassion
and our failures into signs of grace.
Forgive us and make us new
until we become one with the lost,
until we are lost in your love. Amen.

There follows a time for silence or open prayer, concluding with the following words.

Leader   Jesus, good teacher,
you know how to cross boundaries,
to span generations,
to link hand with hand
and to turn the unwanted into a faithful band.

All   We turn to you.

When we make a wall, you build a bridge,
when we draw a line, you step across,
when we shut the door, you stand in our midst,
when we fear, you say 'Do not be afraid.'

Leader   Good teacher, show us the way to that eternal life
in which all are healed through your cross
and made anew by your resurrection. Amen.

Chorus   '*Thuma mina, thuma mina*' ('Send me, Jesus, send me, Jesus')
(or another suitable song)

Renewal of commitment to fight stigma

All   We uphold the dignity and worth of all people, for all people are made in the image of God. We commit ourselves to working for an end to the stigmatization that denies worth and destroys hope, and we join with all our brothers and sisters living with HIV in proclaiming God's grace and love.

Prayer

All   Eternal God,
by whose power we are created
and by whose love we are redeemed:
guide and strengthen us by your Spirit
that we may give ourselves to your service
and live this day in love for you and one another;
through Jesus Christ our Lord. Amen.

Dismissal

Leader	The way is long;
All	**let us go together.**
Leader	The way is difficult;
All	**let us help each other.**
Leader	The way is joyful;
All	**let us share it.**
Leader	The way is Christ's, for Christ is the way,
All	**let us follow.**
	The way is open before us.
	Let us go;
	with the love of God,
	the grace of Christ
	and the communion of the Holy Spirit.
	Amen.

Christmas

At Christmas we celebrate God's love for the world. Through the birth of his son, Jesus Christ, God came to be one of us, sharing in our hopes and fears, our sorrows and our joys. Christmas is a time to celebrate life, and to reflect on what Jesus' promise to bring life in all its fullness means to us and to the millions of people around the world who live in poverty.

THE GIFT OF LIFE

Preparation

Before the service, position a Christmas crib in a prominent place and give each person, on arrival, enough pipe-cleaners of one colour – red, yellow, brown, black and white – to make a pipe-cleaner baby.

Introduction

Leader   At a time when we celebrate the birth of Jesus and the fullness of life God promises through the incarnation, this service celebrates the gift of life and explores the prospects, hopes and dreams of today's children. Let us begin by thanking God for the gift of our own life, with words from Psalm 139.

Leader   O Lord you have searched me and know me;
All   **you know when I sit down and when I rise up.**

Leader   You discern my thoughts from far away.
            You search out my path and my lying down;
All   **you are acquainted with all my ways.**

Leader   For you formed my inward parts;
            You knit me together in my mother's womb.
All   **I praise you, for I am fearfully and wonderfully made.**

Leader   My frame was not hidden from you,
            when I was being made in secret;

All   **when I was woven in the depths of the earth.**

Leader   Your eyes beheld my unformed substance;

All   **in your book were written all my days.**

Leader   How weighty to me are your thoughts, O God!

All   **How vast is the sum of them!**

Leader   I try to count them – they are more than the sand.

All   **As I wake up in the morning I know I am with you.**

Hymn or song

Opening prayer

Leader   Mother God
           in whose arms are held
           all who cry out to you:
           teach me to open my heart, my home,
           even when I have little to give,
           to make room for all your children
           and give them space to grow.
           Amen.

Leader   During the course of this service 10,000 children will be born in the world. Of them, 2,000 will be born into abject poverty and a handful into breathtaking wealth. One fifth of the world's population will be deprived of the basic necessities of life.

           In a world where all people belong to God and are of equal value, how can we allow this to happen?

Reflecting on equality and inequality

The making of pipe-cleaner babies

There now follows a time for everyone to make a pipe-cleaner baby. During this time, meditative music may be played.

Leader   As we make our pipe-cleaner babies, let us reflect how each one will be made of the same materials, but unique, a

reminder both of each person's individual worth and of our
equality in the sight of God.

Leader   Beautiful human child
Brought to life
By the greatest miracle

Born to the rhythms of nature
Beyond control

You lie, curled
Perfect in your newness
Totally dependent

Unknowing of circumstance
Of future
Of possibility
Of doors already shut

What will your life bring?

Hymn or song

Reading

Reader   As for your birth, on the day you were born your naval cord
was not cut, nor were you washed with water to cleanse
you, nor rubbed with salt, nor wrapped in cloths. No eye
pitied you, to do any of these things for you out of compassion for you; but you were thrown out in the open field, for
you were abhorred on the day you were born.
    I passed by you, and saw you flailing about in your blood.
As you lay in your blood I said to you, 'Live!'

Ezekiel 16. 4–6

Let us imagine . . .

Leader   Let us imagine two children born today, one in the UK and
one in Mali in Africa. We will call them Grace and Sarah. I
wonder, what does life have to offer them?

Reader 1   Baby Sarah, born here today, has a one in 166 chance of
dying before her first birthday.

Reader 2   Baby Grace, born in Africa today, has a one in 10 chance of dying before her first birthday.

Leader   No eye pitied you, but I said to you, 'Live'.

Silence

Reader 1   One in 143 of baby Sarah's friends will die before their fifth birthday.

Reader 2   One in five of baby Grace's friends will die before their fifth birthday.

Leader   No eye pitied you, but I said to you, 'Live'.

Silence

Reader 1   Sarah will have a one in 7,000 chance of dying in child-birth.

Reader 2   Grace will have a one in 15 chance of dying in childbirth.

Leader   No eye pitied you, but I said to you, 'Live'.

Silence

Reader 1   Sarah will die in her late 70s.

Reader 2   Grace probably will not live to 50.

Leader   No eye pitied you, but I said to you, 'Live'.

Silence

Prayer of Confession

Leader   God,
You chose to let your child be born in poverty
and of doubtful parentage
in an occupied country with unstable rulers.
You chose to let him risk death in a dirty stable
after a long journey by a pregnant teenager.
You chose to let him grow up poor, and in danger,
and misunderstood by those who loved him.

While the rich are still full
and it is the poor who are sent away empty,
help us, lest we, in our ignorance or anger
walk away, from those who have no choice.
Amen

Hymn or song

Reading

Reader   The king of Egypt said to the Hebrew midwives, one of whom was named Shiphrah and the other Puah, 'When you act as midwives to the Hebrew women and see them on the birthstool, if it is a boy, kill him; but if it is a girl she shall live.' But the midwives feared God; they did not do as the king of Egypt commanded them, but they let the boys live. So the king of Egypt summoned the midwives and said to them, 'Why have you done this and allowed the boys to live?' The midwives said to Pharaoh, 'Because the Hebrew woman are not like the Egyptian women; for they are vigorous and give birth before the midwife comes to them.' So God dealt with the midwives; and the people multiplied and became very strong. And because the midwives feared God he gave them families.

Exodus 1.15–21

Stories from Christian Aid partners

Leader   Afghanistan has the second highest maternal mortality rate in the world. Every 30 minutes an Afghan woman dies in childbirth. In addition to this, one in four children in Afghanistan will die before their fourth birthday. The Skills Training and Rehabilitation Society (STARS) supports vulnerable groups of Afghan women. Nazoko is 22 and has just had her second child. She received training and educational support from STARS. She says:

Reader   STARS told me that if I am not healthy then the child will not be healthy. They told me what foods I should eat, like vegetables and fruit, and told me it was important that I get a lot of rest. They also told me about diseases that babies can get – and how to treat them and protect against them.

Leader Bangladesh is one of the poorest countries in the world, in rural villages there is little or no health care and one in 10 children die before their fifth birthday.

In the village of Chalkkusumba, a nutrition centre has transformed Shafiqul's life. Just six months ago, Shafiqul was underweight for his two years and not thriving at all. His parents were at a loss with what to do with him and had no one to turn to for help. Chalkkusumba is a small village that has not had any outside support. Christian Aid partner the Christian Commission for Development in Bangladesh (CCDB) helped the community establish a village forum and worked with it to identify and address its concerns.

Having seen that many of the children in the village were malnourished, CCDB encouraged the community to establish a nutrition programme for children under five years of age. CCDB weighed 55 children and identified 20 children that were in a particularly vulnerable condition, including Shafiqul. For six months, Shafiqul and the other children received a nutritious diet of vegetables, pulses and rice. The children's weight was carefully monitored and by the end of the programme all had shown a marked improvement, with six achieving their target weight for their age.

Among them all, Shafiqul has shown the most dramatic improvement. He is a walking and talking example to other parents of how a healthy balanced diet can transform a listless infant into a lively and inquisitive toddler.

Responding to God's call

Intercessions with sung response

Leader Holding your pipe-cleaner baby as a symbol of children throughout the world, let us pray together for their care. As our prayers draw to a close, we will place our figures in the Christmas crib as a symbol of both their vulnerability and God's presence with us.

As we hold these figures in our hands, let us pray for those children whose lives will be held in our hands.

We pray that, as they start out, they will know life in all its abundance, that they will be safe from disease, live long lives, have many friends and enjoy the good gifts that God has given them.

Take time to remember the children who are precious to you.

Silence

Sung response

Leader As a sign that we are called to care for other children, in far off places, whom we do not know and will never meet, exchange the figure that you hold with one that your neighbour has made.

We pray for ourselves, committing us to follow in the footsteps of Shiphrah and Puah, to stand up to injustice and to cruelty and to act to save the lives of children who are poor and vulnerable. We pray for Nazoko in Afghanistan and for Shafiqul in Bangladesh that they will continue to care for the health and life of children in their care.

Take time to remember them.

Silence

Sung response

Leader Let us pray for God's children and then, as we sing, let us place our pipe-cleaner figures into the crib and commit our children to God's care.

We pray for all God's children, that they may know a world where all are treated equally because each person is infinitely precious to God. We pray for the time when poverty will become a thing of the past and all children can share in the riches of play, learning and laughter. We long for the time when children will have a future without fear. We say to all children everywhere, 'Live'!

During the singing of the sung response, several times over, each person places their pipe-cleaner figure in the crib.

Sung response

Closing prayer

Leader   We prayer together:
All   **Christ, our God,**
           you were born into our world
           a vulnerable child,
           subject to poverty and disease,
           religious and political harassment.
           In your name,
           let us cry freedom
           for your children
           now, at this time,
           and through all generations.
           Amen.

Closing hymn or song

Epiphany

At Epiphany, we recall the journey of the magi to find the Christ-child and reflect on God's revelation to all people both through our own journeys and the encounters we have along the way with the person of Jesus, the Church and the people we meet in our daily lives.

JOURNEYS

Preparation

Display several maps of the world and the UK around the worship area and have sufficient marker-pens for each person to use.

Welcome and introduction

Gathering prayer

Leader	Creator of the world, eternal God,
All	**we have come from many places**
	for a little while.

Leader	Redeemer of humanity, God-with-us,
All	**we have come with all our differences,**
	seeking common ground.

Leader	Spirit of unity, go-between-God,
All	**we have come on journeys of our own,**
	to a place where journeys meet.

Leader	So here, in this place of meeting,
	let us take time together.
	For when paths cross and pilgrims gather,
	there is much to share and celebrate.
All	**In your name, three-in-one God,**
	pattern of community. Amen.

Gathering song

Prayer

Leader	Bless to me, O God,
All	**the earth beneath my feet.**
Leader	Bless to me, O God,
All	**the path whereon I go.**
Leader	Bless to me, O God,
All	**the journey of my desiring.**
Leader	Thou Evermore of evermore,
All	**bless thou to me this hour.**

Reading

Reader   When Pharaoh let the people go, God did not lead them by way of the land of the Philistines, although that was nearer; for God thought, 'If the people face war, they may change their minds and return to Egypt.' So God led the people by the roundabout way of the wilderness toward the Red Sea. The Israelites went up out of the land of Egypt prepared for battle. And Moses took with him the bones of Joseph who had required a solemn oath of the Israelites, saying, 'God will surely take notice of you, and then you must carry my bones with you from here.'

    They set out from Succoth, and camped at Etham, on the edge of the wilderness. The Lord went in front of them in a pillar of cloud by day, to lead them along the way, and in a pillar of fire by night, to give them light, so that they might travel by day and by night. Neither the pillar of cloud by day nor the pillar of fire by night left its place in front of the people.

Exodus 13.17–22

Time for reflection

Leader   In a few moments quiet, pick out one journey in your life that stands out as being particularly significant. It doesn't have to be a long journey or a particularly adventurous one; but just one that has made a difference to you. Then hold that journey in your mind as we move into song.

Silence

Song

Mapping our journeys

Leader   Using the pens provided, everyone is invited to come and mark their journey on one of the maps displayed. If it was a very short journey, just put a dot in the appropriate place. These maps will act as a focal reminder of the variety of journeys we make as we reflect further on their significance.

Reflective music or singing while people mark their journeys on the map. When everyone has returned to their seats all join in the following prayer.

All   Lord of these roads, Lord of every road,
from whom we have come, in whom we move,
to whom we shall return:
recreate this journey in us as a pilgrimage,
with the power of the Father to protect the memory,
with the love of Jesus to transform the hardship,
with the light of the Spirit to enrich the learning.
And so may the road we have taken lead into you,
until we meet at the end of life's travelling
in life and love eternal. Amen.

Reflective questions

Leader   Here are five questions to help us reflect on the significance of our chosen journey. There will be a time of quiet between each one to give us time to think.

1   What physical things did you bring back from your journey? Perhaps photos, souvenirs, work, people, an illness even?

2   What means of transport did you use? Foot, train, bus, car, plane or boat? Perhaps you used several different modes of transport. How did these shape your memories of the journey?

3   What intangible things did you bring back? Sights that have lodged in your mind, perhaps? Or smells – things you tasted; sounds – things you heard; feelings that won't go away?

4 Were there times on the journey when you were aware, either then or in retrospect, of confronting God – perhaps in the events that happened, the sights you took in, the people who crossed your path? Were all these encounters with God good news? Have they changed you in any way; might they change you in any way?

5 What do you now know about 'being alive' that you didn't know before?

Song

Meeting other people on their journeys

Leader   Let us listen to the stories of other people's journeys and who and what they have enountered along the way.

Reader 1   In Burma, the State Peace and Development Council – that's what the military government calls itself – is accused of inflicting torture and forced labour on the Karenni people. Hundreds of thousands have been forced to flee their homes. Tu Lar Paw is one of them. She had to leave her job as a science teacher and risk the treacherous journey to the refugee camps on the border of Thailand. Four of her seven children died.

On the border, the Thailand Burmese Border Consortium, a partner of Christian Aid, helps to create self-governing bodies to manage the village-style camps. They are home to thousands like Tu Lar Paw. She became head teacher of the school for refugee children and Chair of the Karenni Refugee Committee, working to bring justice out of suffering in one of these camps.

Reader 2   Haiti and the Dominican Republic share an island, but there are severe prejudices between the two nations. Thousands of Haitians make their way to the Dominican Republic in the hope of finding work, but when they get there they find themselves at the bottom of the pile, with no access to health or education services, and without legal rights. Haitians who may have lived in the Dominican Republic for two generations can be forcibly removed and repatriated with nothing but the clothes they are wearing.

The Jesuit Refugee Service, a partner of Christian Aid,

lobbies on behalf of those whose lives have been completely disrupted by forced journeys. Simila Nest says, 'When I arrived at the border I had nothing. Someone told me there was an organization that helped people who were repatriated. They gave me some food and shelter, and a small loan to start a business. I sell candy – it is not much but the best I can do. My family does not know where I am. I have not seen them since 1997.'

Prayer

Leader   Lord of the journey,
we ask for your protection on all who have fled their homes.
Give them strength on their journeys and grant that they
    may find places of compassion at which to rest.
Ease their fear as they throw in their lot with strangers
and keep alive their vision of returning to a secure and
    welcoming home. Amen.

Our Epiphany challenge

Reading

Reader   This is what the Lord says: 'Stand at the crossroads and look. Ask for the ancient paths, seek out where the good way is, and walk in it, and you will find rest for your souls.' Hear the word of the Lord, all you who come through these gates to worship. Learn the lesson of the paths on which you have travelled and reform your ways, and you will live securely in this place. Deal with each other justly, do not oppress the refugee, the fatherless or the widow, and do not shed innocent blood. Journey in all the ways I command you, that all may go well with you.

Adapted from Jeremiah 6.16 and 7.1–6

Prayer for our continuing journey

All   God be with us in every pass,
Jesus be with us on every hill,
Spirit be with us on every stream, headland, ridge and lawn,
each sea and land, each moor and meadow,

each landing down, each rising up,
in the trough of the waves, on the crest of the air,
each step of the journey we go.

Blessing

Leader   May the Lord watch over you;
May he prevent your foot from slipping on the journey;
May the Lord be the shade at your right hand;
May the Lord keep you from all harm;
May he watch over your life;
May the Lord watch over your coming and going
both now and for evermore. Amen.

Song

Prayer of commitment

All   All the past we leave behind,
And we take up the task eternal,
And the burden, and the lesson,
Conquering,
holding,
daring,
venturing,
So we go the unknown ways –
Pioneers, O pioneers!

From 'Pioneers, O pioneers!' by Walt Whitman

Lent, Holy Week and Easter

Lent

In our busy world, Lent provides us with an opportunity to stand back, to enter into the wilderness with Jesus and to take time to reflect upon the patterns of our lives. In a spirit of repentance, we are called to acknowledge the wrongs that we have done and our complicity in many of the injustices in the world. And in a spirit of renewal, we are given the space to reorder our priorities and make choices that reflect the bias of God to the poor and marginalized. It is a time to begin again, in the light of the reconciling love and healing grace of God.

MAKING CHOICES

Preparation

Around one area of the worship space, distribute 200 envelopes, each containing a negligible amount of money – in total, £10. On the back of each envelope write the following:

> For if the eagerness is there, the gift is acceptable according to what one has – not according to what one does not have. I do not mean that there should be relief for others and pressure on you, but it is a question of a fair balance between your present abundance and their need, so that their abundance may be for your need, in order that there may be a fair balance. As it is written,
>
> 'The one who had much did not have too much,
> and the one who had little did not have too little.'
>
> *2 Corinthians 8.12–15*

On the other side of the room distribute just 20 envelopes and put £10 in one of them. On the back of the 20 envelopes, write:

'For nothing is hidden that will not be disclosed, nor is anything secret that will not become known and come to light. Then pay attention to how you listen; for to those who have, more will be given; and from those who do not have, even what they seem to have will be taken away.'

Luke 8.17–18

Opening sentences

Leader	God presides in the great assembly.
All	**He is God above all gods.**

Leader	'Defend the cause of the weak,' says the Lord.
All	**'Maintain the rights of the poor.'**

Leader	'Rescue the needy and oppressed,' says the Lord.
All	**'Deliver the world from all that is wicked.'**

Leader	Rise up, O God, and bring the earth justice!
All	**For the nations are yours, and yours alone.**

Psalm 82

Hymn or song

Introduction

Leader   During this service, we are going to give away money to rich people. Why? Because we can! We live in a country where most of us have endless choice; choice which gives us a great deal of control over our lives. Many of us, though not all, can choose to protect ourselves and our families. We can insure ourselves against floods. We can put aside savings to ensure that we will not be destitute in old age. We can make plans for our homes and families in confidence that we will not have to flee them because of conflict. And we can give away money if we choose to.

     Yet many people around the world are so poor that they have little control over their lives and can make few meaningful choices. During Lent let us reflect on our lives, praying

33

for people who cannot make meaningful choices, and for ourselves as we make so many.

Let us start with a reading from Ecclesiastes:

Reading

Reader Enjoy life! Whatever your hand finds to do, do with your might; for there is no work or thought or knowledge or wisdom in Sheol (in the grave) to which you are going. Again I saw that under the sun the race is not to the swift, nor the battle to the strong, nor bread to the wise, nor riches to the intelligent, nor favour to the skillful; but time and chance happen to them all.

Ecclesiastes 9.10–11

Reflection

Leader Think about the choices you have made since you woke up this morning, choices concerning simple things perhaps – food, clothes, hygiene, how to spend the day. Think how your life has developed so that these choices are available to you.

 Be thankful!

Silence

What are the bigger choices you have made in the last year? Perhaps decisions concerning work, leisure, friendships, faith, how you spend your money. You will have had more control over some decisions than others, but all will have had choices attached to them.

 Be thankful!

Silence

Think back further in your life. What have been the major crossroads at which you decided to go one way or another? They may have involved education, or careers, location or relationships. Some of the choices you made may have been difficult. They may not have been good, even, and sometimes circumstances may have taken decision-making out of your control.

Reflect on the route God has taken you on. This may raise complex emotions, and it may not be enough to say . . . be thankful!

Silence

Prayer

Leader	We say together:
All	Creator God,
	give us a heart
	of thankfulness for simple things:
	love and laughter,
	bread and wine,
	tales and dreams.
	Fill our lives with green and growing hope,
	make us a people of justice,
	whose song is Alleluia,
	and whose name breathes life.
	Amen.

PACSA

Hymn or song

Story

Leader	The story we are going to hear tells how a girl in a poor country regained a measure of control over her life, partly through a vital contribution of Christian Aid money. But, in part, also, as a result of a random and unpredictable accident. Nevertheless, good has come out of both of them.
Reader	Anjali is not sure how old she is but thinks she is about 16. She lives in a remote rural area in Andhra Pradesh, India. Her parents died when she was young and Anjali was sent to work as a domestic when she was just seven years old. Every day, she would get up early to fetch water, cook food, wash up and look after the household's children. Anjali found it hard that the children went to school while she missed out on an education, and when she thought about it, it made her cry.

One day some money went missing in the house. Anjali was accused of stealing it and was fired from her job. She returned home to live with her grandmother, whom she didn't even recognize.

Christian Aid partner the Deccan Development Society (DDS) were helping to create a *sangham* (or women's group) in the village. The women in the group saw that Anjali was not being educated and persuaded her grandmother to send her to the Green School, which is run by DDS.

The majority of the 150 children at the Green School are the first in their families to learn to read and write. All of them have been working. Like Anjali, they have never been to school before or have dropped out of local schools.

When Anjali joined school she could barely write her name or read. She now loves to read poetry, is fast catching up on all the years of school that she has missed and has begun to dream big dreams of college and dressmaking in the future.

Prayer

Leader One of the Bible's great songs of confidence in God not only speaks of his knowledge of every slightest chance and change, but also of the need for each individual, and for the world, to be rid of the human sin that allows injustice and inequality to thrive:

Leader O Lord, you have searched me and you know me.
All **You know when I sit and when I rise.**
Leader If I settle on the far side of the sea,
All **even there your hand will guide me.**
Leader You created my inmost being.
All **You knit me together in my mother's womb.**
Leader I praise you for your wonderful works.
All **I am fearfully and wonderfully made.**
Leader Before I was made in the secret place,
All **all the days ordained for me were written in your book.**
Leader Search me, O God, and know my heart.
All **Test me and know my thoughts.**

Leader   See if there is any offensive way in me.
All   **And lead me in the way everlasting.**

Based on Psalm 139

Making an active choice

Leader   At this point in the service we are required to make a choice – the kind of choice we make unawares every day.

We can choose one of three things. On this side of the room are 200 envelopes, each of them containing a negligible amount of money – in total, £10. There is also a message on each envelope – a statement about how the world could be.

On the other side of the room are just 20 envelopes. In total, they contain exactly the same amount of money as the total amount in the 200 envelopes. But 19 of the 20 envelopes are empty – all of the £10 is in one envelope. On the back of each envelope is a message about how the world is.

You can now choose to do one of three things: to choose an envelope from either one side of the room or the other – first come first served, or to opt out of the whole exercise and do nothing. This third option, too, will be making a statement – about how we often chose to relate to each other in the world.

Music will be played while you are choosing and to aid reflection on your choice when you have returned to your seats.

Play reflective music while people are making their choice and bring the music to a close once everyone is seated and has had time to reflect

Further reflection

Leader   Christian Aid believes that development in the poorest parts of the world should be a matter of justice, not a matter of chance because our God is not the God of luck but the God who brings order out of chaos, and calls it love and justice.

Listen to a story that Jesus told. It can be found in Luke 19.11–26.

Reader 1 The Kingdom of God will be like a man going on a journey who called his servants and entrusted his property to them. To one he gave five talents of money, to another two talents, and to another one talent, each according to his ability. Then he went on his journey.

The man who had received the five talents went at once and put his money to work and gained five more. So also, the one with the two talents gained two more. But the man who had received the one talent went off, dug a hole in the ground and hid his master's money.

After a long time the master of those servants returned and settled accounts with them. The man who had received the five talents brought the other five.

Reader 2 Master, you entrusted me with five talents. See, I have gained five more.

Reader 3 Well done, good and faithful servant! You have been faithful with a few things;
I will put you in charge of many things. Come and share your master's happiness!

Reader 1 The man with the two talents also came.

Reader 4 Master, you entrusted me with two talents; see, I have gained two more.

Reader 3 Well done, good and faithful servant! You have been faithful with a few things;
I will put you in charge of many things. Come and share your master's happiness!

Reader 1 Then the man who had received the one talent came.

Reader 5 Master, I knew that you are a hard man, harvesting where you have not sown and gathering where you have not scattered seed. So I was afraid and went out and hid your talent in the ground. See, here is what belongs to you.

Reader 3 You wicked, lazy servant! So you knew that I harvest where I have not sown and gather where I have not scattered seed? Well then, you should have put my money on deposit with the bankers, so that when I returned I would have received it back with interest. Take the talent from him and give it to the one who has the ten talents.

Reader 1 Jesus went on to say: To everyone who has been given much, much will be expected.

Hymn or song

Prayers

Leader Whatever money you have, find a use for it so that you can say, 'The Kingdom of God will be like this.' Our challenge is to use our money, however little or much, to make God's kingdom on earth come closer.

A prayer for our unequal world:

Reader God of justice, we lift before you Anjali and all who are trafficked and trapped as bonded labourers, young and old. We pray that they and all who are enslaved by poverty may be released to make choices.

God of destiny, we lift before you ourselves, so often burdened by choices and possibilities. We pray for the release that will allow us to choose wisely.

God of freedom, we ask this in your name who, for all our sakes, freely chose to take the nature of a slave, and became obedient to death, that we may choose life. Amen.

And now, in the final choice of the service, we say together:

All   I do not choose wealth;
       I do not choose poverty –
       I choose liberty.
       I do not choose merriment;
       I do not choose misery –
       I choose life.
       I do not choose success;
       I do not choose failure –
       I choose to follow Christ. Amen.

Hymn or song

Prayer

Leader	Who can lead me forward into purpose?
All	**O God help me.**
Leader	Who can lead me up into faith?
All	**O God help me.**
Leader	Who can lead me on into courage?
All	**O God help me.**
Leader	Who can lead me out into meaning?
All	**O God help me.**
Leader	How can I be wise with my choices when time and chance happen to us all?
All	**Save us and help us, we humbly pray, O God. Amen.**

Blessing

Leader	Blessed be the One God;
	Blessed be the mystery;
	Blessed be the freedom;
	Blessed be the certainty;
	Let the blessing of God lead us out from here
	to do good with all that he has placed in our hands,
	and all upon which we have chanced.
All	Amen.

A SHORT SERVICE OF REPENTANCE, RECONCILIATION AND HEALING

After the brutality and injustice of apartheid, many South Africans are still hurting and looking for healing, forgiveness and reconciliation. This short liturgy from South Africa offers a safe space for people weighed down by their stories, to be reconciled to their past and to be healed in order to embrace the future and move on.

Call to worship

| Leader | The world belongs to God, |
| All | **the earth and all its people.** |

| Leader | How good and how lovely it is |
| All | **to live together in unity.** |

Leader	Love and faith come together,
All	**justice and peace join hands.**

Leader	If the Lord's disciples keep silent,
All	**these stones would shout aloud.**

Leader	Lord, open our lips
All	**and our mouths shall proclaim your praise.**

The Iona Community

Confession

Leader Merciful God, in your goodness, forgive us our sins against the unity of your family. Make us one in heart and one spirit. Remove the blindness of the heart and mind. Forgive us our wrongdoing and reconcile us to yourself. We ask this through Christ, our Lord.

All **Amen.**

Old Testament reading

Reader In the year that King Uzziah died, I saw the Lord sitting on a throne, high and lofty; and the hem of his robe filled the temple. Seraphs were in attendance above him; each had six wings: with two they covered their faces, and with two they covered their feet, and with two they flew. And one called to another and said: 'Holy, holy, holy is the LORD of hosts; the whole earth is full of his glory.' The pivots on the thresholds shook at the voices of those who called, and the house filled with smoke. And I said: 'Woe is me! I am lost, for I am a man of unclean lips, and I live among a people of unclean lips; yet my eyes have seen the King, the LORD of hosts!' Then one of the seraphs flew to me, holding a live coal that had been taken from the altar with a pair of tongs. The seraph touched my mouth with it and said: 'Now that this has touched your lips, your guilt has departed and your sin is blotted out.' Then I heard the voice of the Lord saying, 'Whom shall I send, and who will go for us?' And I said, 'Here am I; send me!' And he said, 'Go and say to this people:

41

"Keep listening, but do not comprehend; keep looking,
but do not understand."
Make the mind of this people dull, and stop their ears,
and shut their eyes so that they may not look with their eyes,
and listen with their ears, and comprehend with their minds,
and turn and be healed.'

Isaiah 6.1–10

Cleansing with water

*The congregation may be invited either to wash their hands in a basin
of water or be sprinkled with water as a symbol of cleansing.*

New Testament reading

Reader From now on, therefore, we regard no one from a human
point of view; even though we once knew Christ from a
human point of view, we know him no longer in that way. So
if anyone is in Christ, there is a new creation: everything old
has passed away; see, everything has become new! All this
is from God, who reconciled us to himself through Christ,
and has given us the ministry of reconciliation; that is, in
Christ God was reconciling the world to himself, not count-
ing their trespasses against them, and entrusting the message
of reconciliation to us. So we are ambassadors for Christ,
since God is making his appeal through us; we entreat you
on behalf of Christ, be reconciled to God. For our sake he
made him to be sin who knew no sin, so that in him we
might become the righteousness of God.

2 Corinthians 5.16–21

Healing

*The congregation may anoint each other with oil, making the sign of
the cross on a neighbour's forehead as a symbol of God's forgiveness
and healing touch.*

Gospel reading

Reader So when you are offering your gift at the altar, if you remember that your brother or sister has something against you,
leave your gift there before the altar and go; first be recon-

ciled to your brother or sister, and then come and offer your
gift.

Matthew 5.23–24

The Peace

Leader   How very good and pleasant it is
        when kindred live together in unity!
    It is like the precious oil on the head,
        running down upon the beard,
    on the beard of Aaron,
        running down over the collar of his robes.
    It is like the dew of Hermon,
        which falls on the mountains of Zion.
    For there the Lord ordained his blessing,
        life for evermore.

Psalm 133

    Go in the peace of Christ.
All   **Thanks be to God.**

*The congregation is invited to offer one another a sign of peace before
departing.*

Holy Week

In Holy Week, Christians follow Jesus' journey from his triumphal entry into Jerusalem on a donkey, where he was feted with palm branches and heralded as king, to his betrayal at the last supper and the mockery of his trial and death on the cross. It is a week in which we are reminded of the fickleness of human nature and our own capacity for evil, in contrast to the constancy and self-giving love of Christ.

Palm Sunday

FINDING OUR VOICE – NO TO VIOLENT CRIME

On Palm Sunday when we remember Jesus' entry into Jerusalem to the waving of palm branches, it is traditional in many churches for the Passion narrative to be read. Then we hear how shouts of 'Hosanna' quickly turn to 'Crucify him'. The narrative retelling the events of Palm Sunday to Good Friday is a sobering account of the power of mob rule and our capacity for cruelty. It therefore seems fitting that Palm Sunday should serve as a reminder that violent crime is never an answer.

Below is a shortened version of a call to end violent crime made by a number of South African Church Leaders in 2006. It is a call that speaks to communities anywhere seeking to respond to violence in its midst.

We are all the key to building peace in a situation of violent crime. In our endeavours to reclaim our human dignity, we need to live out our common values, have compassion for others and care for one another.

We call on families to exercise their calling as units of peace and moral integrity. We call on our youth to consider the future and their education, to choose now to become ambassadors of peace.

We call upon perpetrators, as a true act of responsible citizenship, to come clean and confess their criminal acts, hand over their weapons, stop dealing in drugs, cease destructive behaviour, and instead join us in embracing the common human dignity that we all share.

We call on victims, onlookers and survivors to break the silence. Report violent crime and harm done to you and your loved ones. We stand with you. We stand together as one, and our dignity binds us to one another beyond any measure of threat and aggression.

Call to worship

Leader   This is the day that the Lord has made; let us rejoice and be glad in it.

All   **Our hearts are glad as we rejoice in the one who comes in the name of the Lord.**

Confession and absolution

Leader   It seems such a distance from the first Palm Sunday when Jesus entered Jerusalem to the shouts of the crowd; welcomed as a king, yet riding on a donkey; greeted with cheers and acclamations that were so soon to turn to jeers and condemnation. From this side of the resurrection, we may confidently believe that we could never have been part of the baying crowd – but would we, if we had been there?

Silent reflection

Leader   Lord Jesus Christ, when our words and actions reflect a reluctance to confess you publicly as Lord of our lives:

All   **Forgive us.**

Leader   When we fear that others would see humility as weakness or some kind of defect in our character:

All   **Forgive us.**

Leader   When we have betrayed your love for us through our lack of love for you, for others, and for ourselves:

All   **Forgive us.**

Leader   When we find ourselves lacking respect for life and the lives of others:

All   **Forgive us.**

Leader   Lord Jesus Christ, fix your mind in us and remake us in your likeness; empty us of all that hinders us from following you to where pain and suffering, exploitation and injustice exist.

All   Gracious and loving God, empower us with the Holy Spirit
so that our lives continually glorify you and our tongues forever confess Jesus as Lord. Help us to respect and love one
another. This we pray in Jesus' name. Amen.

Assurance of forgiveness

Leader   Hear the good news: 'Jesus, though he was in the form of
God, did not count equality with God as something to be
exploited, but emptied himself, taking the form of a slave . . .
and became obedient to the point of death, even death on a
cross.'

Philippians 6.7a, 8b

All   **Thanks be to God!**

Listening to God's Word

Old Testament reading

Reader   The Lord GOD has given me
the tongue of a teacher,
that I may know how to sustain
the weary with a word.
Morning by morning he wakens—
wakens my ear
to listen as those who are taught.
The Lord GOD has opened my ear,
and I was not rebellious,
I did not turn backwards.
I gave my back to those who struck me,
and my cheeks to those who pulled out the beard;
I did not hide my face
from insult and spitting.

The Lord GOD helps me;
therefore I have not been disgraced;
therefore I have set my face like flint,
and I know that I shall not be put to shame;
he who vindicates me is near.
Who will contend with me?

Let us stand up together.
Who are my adversaries?
Let them confront me.
It is the Lord GOD who helps me;
who will declare me guilty?
All of them will wear out like a garment;
the moth will eat them up.

Isaiah 50.4–9a

New Testament reading

Reader   Let the same mind be in you that was in Christ Jesus,
who, though he was in the form of God,
did not regard equality with God
as something to be exploited,
but emptied himself,
taking the form of a slave,
being born in human likeness.
And being found in human form,
he humbled himself
and became obedient to the point of death—
even death on a cross.

Therefore God also highly exalted him
and gave him the name
that is above every name,
so that at the name of Jesus
every knee should bend,
in heaven and on earth and under the earth,
and every tongue should confess
that Jesus Christ is Lord,
to the glory of God the Father.

Philippians 2.5–11

Gospel reading

Reader   The next day the great crowd that had come to the festival heard that Jesus was coming to Jerusalem. So they took
branches of palm trees and went out to meet him, shouting,
'Hosanna! Blessed is the one who comes in the name of the
Lord— the King of Israel!' Jesus found a young donkey and

47

sat on it; as it is written: 'Do not be afraid, daughter of Zion. Look, your king is coming, sitting on a donkey's colt!' His disciples did not understand these things at first; but when Jesus was glorified, then they remembered that these things had been written of him and had been done to him.

John 12.12–16

Address or reflection

Prayers of intercession

Leader   Let us pray for the whole people of God in Christ Jesus, and for all people according to their needs.

Merciful God, through the birth of your Son, you came to be one of us. Born under occupation, you became a refugee. In your life and work you showed bias to the poor and through suffering on the cross, you identified with those who suffer from injustice. We thank you for sharing our joy, our suffering and our pain.

Lord, in your mercy,
All   **hear our prayer.**

Leader   Eternal God, you know the troubles and pains of all your people. We pray for victims of injustice and violence, and for those who have caused their suffering. We pray for young people who despair of the future and all who have lost hope. We pray for the bereaved and all who mourn the loss of loved ones.

Lord, in your mercy,
All   **hear our prayer.**

Leader   Healing God, you touch us with your love. We pray for the recovery of the injured and the rehabilitation of those who live with disability. We pray for politicians and community workers that they may be granted wisdom and courage to search for ways that lead to reconciliation and peace.

Lord, in your mercy,
All   **hear our prayer.**

Leader Living God, you created us in your image. Give us grace to recognize each person's worth and courage to honour each person's human, religious, civil and political rights. Free us from all hatred and bitterness and help us to build a culture of peace, justice and reconciliation.

Lord, in your mercy,
All **hear our prayer.**

Leader Reconciling God, your son preached peace to those who were far off and peace to those who were near. Give peace to your Church, peace among nations, peace in our homes and peace in our hearts.

Merciful God, you are our strength, refuge and hope. Accept our prayers and yearnings in the name of Jesus, our liberator and redeemer.
All **Amen.**

Leader God weeps over this troubled world. God depends on us to work for justice and for peace, to exercise compassion and gentleness, to care for this world and to share its blessings. And so we join in the prayer of yearning that Jesus himself taught us:
All **Our Father, who art in heaven . . .**

Benediction

Leader Go into the world in peace,
committed to working for justice
ready to confront crime and violence,
embraced by the steadfast love of God,
blessed by the humility and courage of Jesus Christ
and filled with the immeasurable power of the Holy Spirit.
Amen.

Maundy Thursday

THE KISS

On Maundy Thursday the Church remembers the Last Supper and Judas' betrayal of Jesus, which reaches its climax with Judas kissing Jesus before Jesus' arrest in the Garden of Gethsamene. This service looks at the symbol of the kiss, the X, exploring its significance and the message it conveys.

Preparation

You will need:

✠ individual world maps, perhaps printed on the back of the service sheets
✠ pens or pencils
✠ a container of oil.

Introduction

Opening responses

Leader	Love and faithfulness meet together;
All	**righteousness and peace kiss each other.**

Leader	Faithfulness springs forth from the earth,
All	**and righteousness looks down from heaven.**

Leader	The Lord will indeed give us what is good,
All	**so our earth will yield its harvest.**

Leader	Righteousness goes before our God,
All	**let justice prepare the way for his steps.**

From Psalm 85

Opening hymn or song

Exploring the kiss

Leader   Love and faithfulness meet together. Righteousness and peace kiss each other. We celebrate love with a kiss. The symbol for a kiss is an X and Xs have more than one meaning.

Reading

Reader 1   Kiss me with the kisses of your mouth, for your love is more delightful than wine. Your name is like perfume poured out. No wonder the maidens adore you! Take me away with you – let us hurry! Bring me into your chambers. If only you were my brother! Then I could kiss you, and no one would scorn me. Place me like a seal over your heart, like a kiss on your arm; for love is as strong as death, its jealousy unyielding as the grave. It burns like blazing fire, like a mighty flame. Many waters cannot quench love; rivers cannot wash it away.

Song of Songs 1.1–4; 8.6–8

Leader   X stands for a kiss.
Reader 1   Exuberance.
Reader 2   Excitement.
Reader 1   Xmas.
Reader 2   Expectation.
Reader 1   Ecstasy.
Reader 2   Existence.
Reader 1   Excellence.
Reader 2   Exodus.
Reader 1   Exhilaration.
Reader 2   Exultation.

Leader   X marks something that is wrong.
Reader 1   Excess.
Reader 2   Extortion.
Reader 1   Expletives.
Reader 2   Exhibitionism.
Reader 1   Exhaustion.
Reader 2   Explosion.
Reader 1   Extinction.
Reader 2   Excuses.

Reader 1   Execution.
Reader 2   X-rated.

Reading

Reader 1   While he was still speaking, Judas, one of the Twelve, arrived.
With him was a large crowd armed with swords and clubs,
sent from the chief priests and the elders of the people. Now
the betrayer had arranged a signal with them: 'The one I kiss
is the man; arrest him.' Going at once to Jesus, Judas said,
'Greetings, Rabbi!' and kissed him. Jesus replied, 'Friend, do
what you came for.' Then the men stepped forward, seized
Jesus and arrested him. With that, one of Jesus' companions
reached for his sword, drew it out and struck the servant of
the high priest, cutting off his ear. 'Put your sword back in
its place,' Jesus said to him, 'for all who draw the sword will
die by the sword.'

Matthew 26.47–52

Leader   This service is called 'Kiss', and its starting point is the X
that we use as a sign of love. And as a sign of many other
things. Where are all the places in life – work, school, home,
entertainment, writing – that you have seen the sign of a
cross used to stand for something?

Silent reflection

Hymn or song

Leader   This service rejoices in God's gift of love to the world – the
gift that is demonstrated in the cross of Christ and celebrated
in his life-giving resurrection; and it helps us to explore how
we give back to God's world the life he has blessed us with.

Readings

Reader 1   Beloved, let us love one another, because love is from God;
everyone who loves is born of God and knows God. Who-
ever does not love does not know God, for God is love. God's
love was revealed among us in this way: God sent his only

Son into the world so that we might live through him. In this is love, not that we loved God but that he loved us and sent his Son to be the atoning sacrifice for our sins. Beloved, since God loved us so much, we also ought to love one another. No one has ever seen God; if we love one another, God lives in us, and his love is perfected in us.

1 John 4.7–12

Reader 2   Words of the 13th-century Christian leader, Bonaventura:

'What kind of man is this, who for our sakes is hanging on the cross, whose suffering causes the rocks themselves to crack and crumble with compassion, whose death brings the dead back to life?

    Let my heart crack and crumble at the sight of him. Let my soul break apart with compassion for his suffering. Let it be shattered with grief at my sins for which he dies. And finally let it be softened with devoted love for him.'

Leader   Knowing that our love is weak, but God's love is limitless, we pray together:

All   **For our lack of love for you,
and our lack of love for one another;
For forgetting the poor,
and forgetting the broken;
For failing to understand the outsider,
and failing to welcome the outcast.
Forgive us, Lord,
and give us grace to change,
so that we may live with the joy that Jesus lived,
and love with the richness that Jesus loved. Amen.**

Hymn or song

Blessing and sending out

Leader   Love and faithfulness meet each other. Righteousness and peace kiss each other. The last minutes of our service recognize that if God's love is to kiss the whole of a needy world, then it must begin with us. So our final act of worship is to

53

ask God's blessing on each other, and to make that blessing as visible as it is real.

You are invited to invoke God's blessing on your neighbour by dipping your finger in the pot of oil that will be passed round and, with it, marking a cross as a kiss on the palm of their hand, saying 'You are blessed by God. Be whole!' – or other appropriate words.

Leaders demonstrate the blessing.

Background music played while oil is passed round for blessing each other.

Hymn or song

The sending out

Leader   As we leave this place,
let us hold in our prayers all people –
waking, sleeping, being born, and dying –
one world, one humanity,
forever changing, forever the same.
Let us go from here as people who have been kissed by God,
secure in the knowledge that goodness will be the master of
    evil,
and eager, in the company of Jesus Christ the righteous
    one,
to walk a bright path through time.

All   The kiss of God on the men and on the women;
the kiss of God on our bodies and on our souls;
the kiss of God on our work and on our leisure;
the kiss of God on our youth and our maturity;
the kiss of God on the rich and on the poor;
the kiss of God on all who cry out to Jesus
today and ever more.
Amen.

Good Friday

THROUGH THE CROSS

On Good Friday Christians remember the crucifixion – Jesus' self-giving on the cross for our redemption. We call to mind our own brokenness and the brokenness of the world that is named in the silence from the cross, and in that silence we hear the unheard voices of those around the world crying out for justice.

Preparation

You will need a simple, wooden processional cross covered with chicken-wire or binding through which flower stems can be fed, as well as flowers for decoration and small hand-held crosses for the congregation.

Call to worship

Leader   Vulnerable Christ, draw us to your cross which brings forgiveness
All   **that we may be cleansed.**

Leader   Crucified Christ, draw us to your cross which brings love
All   **that we may have compassion.**

Leader   Come, let us mourn Christ crucified for us to overcome.

Entrance of the cross

The congregation stand in silence while the cross is brought in. When it has been placed in a central position, the congregation remain standing while a soloist sings 'Were you there when they crucified my Lord?'

Hymn or song

Confession

Leader	God of creation, you made the world
All	**and you saw that it was good.**
Leader	You made us stewards of your creation
All	**yet, in our greed we have created poverty.**
Leader	You heard the cry of your people and delivered them
All	**yet we shut out the poor.**

Silence

Leader	Listening God, we ask your forgiveness.

Leader	Loving Jesus, you came to your own.
	And your own people did not accept you.
	You were in the form of God
All	**yet you emptied yourself, taking the form of a servant.**
Leader	You would not turn stones into bread for yourself
All	**yet you fed the multitudes.**
Leader	You prayed that we might be one
All	**yet we continue to divide rich and poor by our unjust systems.**
Leader	You came that we might have life in abundance.
All	**yet we deny abundant life to the majority.**
	And you say, 'I thirst'.

Silence

Leader	Loving God, we ask your forgiveness.
All	**Forgiving God, we know that you love us and will help us to change.**
	Give us the strength, through the cross of Jesus,
	to overcome our weakness, our apathy and our fear
	that we may be co-creators with you in developing a more just world
	and so make the earth a good home for all. Amen.

Hymn or song

Listening to God's word

Old Testament reading

Reader   Here is my servant, whom I uphold,
my chosen, in whom my soul delights;
I have put my spirit upon him;
he will bring forth justice to the nations.
He will not cry or lift up his voice,
or make it heard in the street;
a bruised reed he will not break,
and a dimly burning wick he will not quench;
he will faithfully bring forth justice.
He will not grow faint or be crushed
until he has established justice in the earth;
and the coastlands wait for his teaching.

Isaiah 42.1–4

New Testament reading

Reader   For the love of Christ urges us on, because we are convinced that one has died for all; therefore all have died. And he died for all, so that those who live might live no longer for themselves, but for him who died and was raised for them.

2 Corinthians 5.14–15

Chorus

Gospel reading

Reader   When he came to Nazareth, where he had been brought up, he went to the synagogue on the sabbath day, as was his custom. He stood up to read, and the scroll of the prophet Isaiah was given to him. He unrolled the scroll and found the place where it was written:
    'The Spirit of the Lord is upon me,
because he has anointed me
to bring good news to the poor.
He has sent me to proclaim release to the captives
and recovery of sight to the blind,
to let the oppressed go free,
to proclaim the year of the Lord's favour.'

And he rolled up the scroll, gave it back to the attendant, and sat down. The eyes of all in the synagogue were fixed on him. Then he began to say to them, 'Today this scripture has been fulfilled in your hearing.'

Luke 4.16–21

Sermon or reflection

The veneration of the cross

Distribution of crosses

The hand-held crosses are given out to the congregation and are held as people pray the prayers of intercession.

Prayers of intercession

Leader   In union with Christ, let us pray that all may receive the benefits of his passion.
We pray for all who suffer the daily struggle that poverty brings.

Lord, through the power of your cross
All   **bring life in all its fullness.**

Leader   We pray for parents who long to educate their children.

Lord, through the power of your cross
All   **bring life in all its fullness.**

Leader   We pray for all who live with the effects of HIV.

Lord, through the power of your cross
All   **bring life in all its fullness.**

Leader   We pray for the healing of communities traumatized by crime.

Lord, through the power of your cross
All   **bring life in all its fullness.**

Leader   We pray that people may work together to build a better life.

Lord, through the power of your cross
All   **bring life in all its fullness.**

Leader   We pray that in all people the desire to share will be stronger than the desire to consume.

Lord, through the power of your cross
All   **bring life in all its fullness.**

Leader   We pray that all people may work together to treasure the earth and nurture the environment.

Lord, through the power of your cross
All   **bring life in all its fullness.**

Leader   We pray that governments may put in place just structures and strive to deliver effective services for all.

Lord, through the power of your cross
All   **bring life in all its fullness.**

Leader   We pray that everywhere churches and NGOs may help to facilitate development that honours the worth of all God's people.

All   **Lord, through the power of your cross**
bring life in all its fullness
that all may be empowered to love and to serve.
Amen.

Procession

The cross is carried in silence around the church or grounds or sur-rounding streets. The congregation follow holding their hand-held crosses. When the procession stops at its destination, the congregation gather around the cross to sing a hymn.

Hymn or song

Flowering of the cross

Members of the congregation are invited to place flowers on or around the cross, as a sign of veneration and to symbolize death giving way to life. When all the flowers have been placed, the congregation are invited to join in an act of commitment.

Act of commitment

Leader	God of love, we commit ourselves to work for a more just world:
All	**where the voice of the poor is heard,** **where the rich share their wealth** **and the lives of both are transformed.**

Leader	God of justice, we commit ourselves to live more just lives:
All	**to consider how the choices we make effect others,** **to be content with enough and** **to spend to live not live to spend.**

Leader	God of life, we commit ourselves to work with others:
All	**to care for the earth,** **to share its resources and** **to make a fairer world for all. Amen.**

Hymn or song

The blessing

Leader	May God, the Creator help us to cherish the earth for the good of all, now and for ever.
	May God, the Redeemer, help us to transform riches for some into blessings for all.
	May the God, the Life-giver help us to work together to make all thing new.
All	Amen.

HOW LONG . . .?

The Approach

Leader	How long must we cry out for help, O Lord?
All	**How long must we cry out for help?**

Leader	When surrounded by wrongdoing and trouble,
All	**how long must we cry out for help?**

Leader	When people cry out, 'Violence',
All	**how long must we cry out for help?**

Leader	When we are surrounded by destruction,
All	**how long must we cry out for help?**

Leader	While judgement is perverted,
All	**how long must we cry out for help?**

Leader	Look at the nations. Be astonished! Be astounded!
All	**How long must we cry out for help?**

Based on Habakkuk 1.2–4

The Word

Reading

Reader　He was despised and rejected by others; a man of suffering and acquainted with infirmity; and as one from whom others hide their faces he was despised, and we held him of no account. Surely he has borne our infirmities and carried our diseases; yet we account him stricken, struck down by God and afflicted. But he was wounded for our transgressions, crushed by our iniquities; upon him was the punishment that made us whole, and by his bruises we are healed.

Isaiah 53.3–5

Voices

Leader　Sebaston, from Malawi, is glad to be alive. He can barely walk and his limbs are paralysed on one side. Although his health is improving now that he is taking anti-retroviral drugs, his wife left him when he was diagnosed. She has subsequently died.

Voice 1　I was despised and rejected.

Silence

Leader   Noma, from South Africa, left her job at the Post Office because she was unable to join the blood donation scheme owing to being HIV-positive. People started to talk about her and the gossip drove her away.

Voice A   I was despised and rejected.

Silence

Sung response   'O Lord, hear my prayer'

Reading

Reader   When the Son of Man comes in his glory, and all the angels with him, then he will sit on the throne of his glory. All the nations will be gathered before him and he will separate people one from another as a shepherd separates the sheep from the goats, and he will put the sheep at his right hand and the goats at the left. Then the King will say to those at his right hand, 'Come you that are blessed by my Father, inherit the Kingdom prepared for you from the foundation of the world; for I was hungry and you gave me food, I was thirsty and you gave me something to drink, I was a stranger and you welcomed me, I was naked and you gave me clothing, I was sick and you took care of me.'

Matthew 25.31–37

Leader   Diane Campbell is a nurse who works with Jamaica Aids Support in Kingston. She says: 'As Christians in church we need to share whatever God has blessed us with. If you see someone with HIV you need to comfort them. If the Church does not show and 'do' love, how can the people know God?'

Voice 3   I was sick and you took care of me.

Silence

Sung response   'O Lord hear my prayer'

The Response

Leader   'Hugging is a warm thing. It is sharing a sense of inner feeling. You may not give people the words they need, but you can still show them how much you care and love them. It is magnificent to touch people who have been rejected. It can bring them peace. I always try to hug people a lot.'

Diane Campbell, nurse

Leader   May the peace of God, which passes all understanding, keep our hearts and minds in the knowledge and love of God in Christ Jesus.
             The peace of the Lord be always with you

All   **and also with you.**

Leader   Let us offer one another a sign of peace.

Closing prayer

Leader   When we are down and helpless,
All   **may your Kingdom come.**
Leader   Where joy is gone and hope abandoned,
All   **may your Kingdom come.**
Leader   Where love is lost and sick folk suffer,
All   **may your Kingdom come.**
Leader   When prejudice triumphs over compassion,
All   **may your Kingdom come.**
Leader   Where Churches fail to bring help and healing,
All   **may your Kingdom come.**
Leader   When our hearts are empty of courage and commitment,
All   **may your Kingdom come.**
Leader   May your Kingdom come.
All   **Amen.**

Easter

Easter is about the joyous proclamation of the resurrection, about the defeat of death by life, and our God-given capacity to rebuild amongst the chaos of destruction and to plant seeds of hope amongst despair. It is the source of hope, new life and new beginnings and it proclaims that things can be different.

ALL THINGS ARE MADE NEW: A SHORT SERVICE OF RENEWAL

The lighting of the Easter candle

A central candle is lit. In some churches this may be the Easter or Paschal candle.

Leader	Behold the Light of God!
All	**The Light that makes all things new.**
Leader	The former things shall not be remembered or come to mind.
All	**God's Light renews us all.**
Leader	Long and long our God has declared it: All things will be made anew!
All	**And God's promises are sure!**
Leader	All the heavens and the earth,
All	**all the seas and dry lands,**
Leader	all the stars and moons,
All	**all have been made new!**
Leader	All the forests and the fields,
All	**all the valleys and the mountains,**
Leader	all the rivers and the lakes,
All	**all have been made new!**
Leader	All the fish and the corals,
All	**all the birds and the beasts,**
Leader	all the worms and the insects,
All	**all have been made new!**
Leader	For God has done it!
All	**God has turned death into life.**

Leader	God has turned brokenness into wholeness.
All	**God has saved his people!**
Leader	Christ is risen!
All	**He is risen indeed!**
Leader	Jesus is alive.
All	**A new world is possible.**

The Readings

Reader 1   If for this life only we have hoped in Christ, we are of all people most to be pitied. But in fact Christ has been raised from the dead, the first fruits of those who have died. For since death came through a human being, the resurrection of the dead has also come through a human being; for as all die in Adam, so all will be made alive in Christ. But each in his own order: Christ the first fruits, then at his coming those who belong to Christ. Then comes the end,when he hands over the kingdom to God the Father, after he has destroyed every ruler and every authority and power. For he must reign until he has put all his enemies under his feet. The last enemy to be destroyed is death.

1 Corinthians 15.19–26

Reader 2   But on the first day of the week, at early dawn, the women came to the tomb, taking the spices that they had prepared. They found the stone rolled away from the tomb, but when they went in, they did not find the body. While they were perplexed about this, suddenly two men in dazzling clothes stood beside them. The women were terrified and bowed their faces to the ground, but the men said to them, 'Why do you look for the living among the dead? He is not here, but has risen. Remember how he told you, while he was still in Galilee, that the Son of Man must be handed over to sinners, and be crucified, and on the third day rise again.' Then they remembered his words, and returning from the tomb, they told all this to the eleven and to all the rest. Now it was Mary Magdalene, Joanna, Mary the mother of James, and the other women with them who told this to the apostles. But these words seemed to them an idle tale, and they did not believe them. But Peter got up and ran to the tomb;

stooping and looking in, he saw the linen cloths by themselves; then he went home, amazed at what had happened.

Luke 24.1–12

The Response

Sung Alleluia

During the singing of the Alleluia, a hand-held candle is lit from the Easter candle and all candles are lit one from the other in a chain effect.

Prayer of renewal

Easter blessing

Dismissal

Leader   Go in the light and peace of Christ.
All   **Thanks be to God.**

The congregation processes out holding their candles. They remain lit until everyone is outside.

FROM SLAVERY TO FREEDOM

The Approach

Leader   At Easter we celebrate our freedom, freedom from sin and all that binds us and holds us back from being the people God created us to be. For some people, the desire for freedom is a physical matter as well as a spiritual one because even in the 21st century, 200 years after slavery was officially abolished, people are still enslaved. They are effectively kept in chains by overwhelming poverty.

This service reminds us of the different ways slavery exists today and how true freedom does not exist in isolation from our neighbours. When anyone is enslaved, the whole of humanity is diminished, and God suffers with us. But restoration is our hope as resurrection is the promise of Easter.

Opening responses

Leader	Praise the Lord, O my soul!
All	**I will praise the Lord as long as I live.**

Leader	Don't put all your trust in people:
All	**When their breath departs, they return to the earth.**

Leader	Happy are those who rely on God
All	**who made heaven, earth, the seas and all that is in them.**

Leader	Who brings justice to the oppressed
All	**and food for the hungry.**

Leader	The Lord sets the prisoners free
All	**and opens the eyes of the blind.**

Leader	The Lord lifts up those who are bowed down
All	**and watches over the strangers in the land.**

Leader	The Lord upholds the orphan and the widow
All	**but brings ruin to the wicked.**

Leader	The Lord will reign forever,
All	**praise the Lord!**

based on Psalm 146

Opening hymn or song

Prayer

Leader	God of life and love,
	You told us to call you Father, Mother.
	You told us to call you Sister, Brother.
	You told us to call you friend.

In the stillness,
we remember that we are loved by you.

We celebrate all the good things you give us
and we rejoice in a new day full of possibilities.

In the stillness,
we give thanks for all we receive from you.

But in a world where poverty, violence and greed,
can extinguish the hopes and freedom of so many,
make us restless until all people can rejoice,
until all can celebrate the gifts of love, liberation and
    fullness of life
that you will for us and all people.
Amen.

The Word

Leader   Slavery, in the sense of one person owning another, is now illegal almost everywhere. Even so, there are an estimated 27 million slaves in the world today. And that number is dwarfed by the hundreds of millions of people who are forced by poverty into situations that enslave them. Like slaves, they have no freedom, no choices, few, if any, rights and little hope.

Song   'Nobody knows the trouble I've seen' (African American spiritual) or another suitable song.

Voices of experience

Voice 1   Hassena Thaj is 24 and lives near Bangalore in India. Her husband left her after the birth of their fourth child and now the only way she can support her children is to be a sex worker.

Voice 2   Four days after the birth of my last child I had to go out on the streets. I would like to take a job that allows me to live with dignity but I need the money so I have to do this or my children go hungry.

Voice 3   No choice, no power, no money, no education, no hope, no future.

Voice 1   Lalithesh is 12 years old and lives in Uttar Pradesh, north India. She works with her parents in a quarry, where the whole family breaks stones for construction. Many children working in the quarry suffer from TB and other respiratory conditions.

Voice 4   My parents break the stones and my job is to separate them from the sandy gravel bits, but sometimes I break stones, too. It makes my hands hurt.

Voice 3   No choice, no power, no money, no education, no hope, no future.

Reading

Reader   If any who are dependent on you become so impoverished that they sell themselves to you, you shall not make them serve as slaves. They shall remain with you as hired or bound labourers. They shall serve with you until the year of the jubilee. Then they and their children with them shall be free from your authority; they shall go back to their own family and return to their ancestral property. For they are my servants, whom I brought out of the land of Egypt; they shall not be sold as slaves are sold. You shall not rule over them with harshness, but shall fear your God.

Leviticus 25.39–43

Song   Repeat the singing of 'Nobody knows the trouble I've seen' or other short meditative song.

Prayer of confession

Leader   God of freedom,
forgive us for being part of a global system
that keeps people in poverty.
Forgive us for being part of a system
that takes away people's choice, power and hope.
Forgive us for the times we have ignored your people
crying out for justice,
crying out for freedom.

All   **Our God forgives all those who truly repent.**
Rise up and live with courage and hope. Amen.

Reading

Reader   For just as the body is one and has many members, and all the members of the body, though many, are one body, so it is with Christ. For in the one Spirit we were all baptized into

one body – Jews or Greeks, slaves or free – and we were all
made to drink of one Spirit. Indeed, the body does not con-
sist of one member but of many . . . The eye cannot say to
the hand, 'I have no need of you,' nor again the head to the
feet, 'I have no need of you.' On the contrary, the members
of the body that seem to be weaker are indispensable . . . If
one member suffers, all suffer together with it; if one member is honoured, all rejoice together with it.

1 Corinthians 12.12–14, 21–22, 26

Voices of promise

Voice 3   Choice, power, money, education, hope, a future.

Voice 1   The SPAD-Milan project in Bangalore, India, is supported
by Christian Aid. It gives sex workers health advice, especially about HIV. It also provides them with condoms and
campaigns for access to medical treatment for all, and
helps women to find alternative ways of supporting their
families.

Voice 5   A few years ago, I tested HIV positive. Since then I have
been raising awareness among clients as an outreach educa-
tor, advocating the use of condoms. I'm part of a support
group, too, which gives me the opportunity to talk to other
women who are positive. My duty is to feed and educate my
children so that they are equipped for the future; hopefully a
future they can determine for themselves.

Voice 3   Choice, power, money, education, hope, a future.

Voice 1   The Safai Karmachari Andolan (SKA) movement in India
is campaigning to bring an end to the practice of manual
scavenging where a section of society is employed to clear
other people's excrement from dry latrines. The so-called
dry latrines are toilets that are not plumbed into a sewer-
age system so waste has to scooped up manually from the
floor and carried away. Manual scavenging is linked to the
caste system and the vast majority of those involved are dalit
women who, at the lowest level of the caste hierarchy, pass
the occupation down from generation to generation. SKA
builds the self-esteem of women and empowers women to
leave the job once and for all.

Voice 6 Bharathi Devi was encouraged by an SKA activist to leave. She says, 'I liked the conversation with her. I had never thought of leaving the work . . . now I motivate other people to do the same. Earlier the money was less, there was no dignity in work. But now, although the work as a domestic is more strenuous, I am able to earn more money, as well as command respect.

Voice 3 Choices, power, money, education, hope, a future.

The Response

Hymn or song

Prayer of intercession

After each bidding, pause for silent reflection during which time a candle is lit.

Leader Liberator Lord,
to everyone who is trapped in slavery, in name or in reality,
All **bring dignity, bring freedom.**

Leader To everyone who has no control over the conditions of
their work,
All **bring empowerment, bring freedom.**

Leader To everyone who is trapped by their lack of rights,
All **bring hope, bring freedom.**

Leader To everyone who is trapped in poverty by the unfair way
the world is run,
All **bring life, bring freedom.**

Leader And to those who support people enslaved by poverty, help
them to
All **bring a future, bring freedom.**
Amen.

Hymn or song

Blessing

Sending out

Leader   God is calling us; God is sending us out in the light of the resurrection.
Let us say together:

All   **The Spirit of the Lord is upon us.**
He has anointed us to bring good news to the poor.
He has sent us to proclaim release to the captives
and recovery of sight to the blind,
to set the oppressed free
and to proclaim that this is the time God has chosen!

Pentecost

At Pentecost, Christians celebrate the coming of the Holy Spirit: the Spirit of God that transformed a disparate group of disciples into a community of believers fired up to proclaim the good news of Jesus Christ and which continues to energize and give shape to the Church today. The drama of the first Pentecost is rich in imagery, conveying the power of the Spirit and its unifying force. For this reason, Pentecost is closely associated with ecumenical endeavour – the desire for all Christians to be united as members of the body of Christ committed to the self-giving service of others.

COME, HOLY SPIRIT

Preparation

Each person will need a tongue of flame, preferably cut from red, orange or yellow paper, and something to write with. These can be handed out as people come in. During the service these will be pinned to a board to make a Pentecostal fire.

There is also an opportunity for a video to be shown illustrating Christian Aid's work.

Welcome

Opening responses

Leader   Come, Holy Spirit.
All   **Come, Lord of life.**

Leader   You bring each new day alive with possibility.
All   **You fill creation with vitality and hope.**

Leader	You give each human being great potential.
All	**You inspire people to transform the world.**

Leader	Come, Holy Spirit, and enter our worship.
All	**Come, Lord of life, and infuse our lives.**

Song or hymn of gathering and praise

Introduction

Leader   In our worship we celebrate the coming of the Holy Spirit to a needy world and explore how she inspires the work of Christian Aid and its supporters, and empowers people in poor communities throughout the world.

Prayer of praise

Leader   Boundless God,
we praise you for your transforming love,
poured onto your disciples on the day of Pentecost,
and freely offered to us now.
We praise you for your Son,
who, in his words and his actions, brought good news to
       the poor.
We praise you for the Spirit who changes lives,
and for the many lives changed through Christian Aid.
Give us open hands and hearts to receive the gift of your
       Holy Spirit,
and open eyes and ears to perceive your Spirit at work in
       the world today.
We ask this in Jesus' name.
Amen.

Prayer of confession

Leader   Creating God, we confess our role in damaging your
       creation.
Loving God, we ask you to forgive us for forgetting our
       global neighbours.
Redeeming God, we pray to be free of the sin which
       burdens us.

All	**Lord, have mercy.**

Leader	May the wind and flames of Pentecost disturb our complacency, awaken our sense of responsibility and kindle our imagination, give us confidence to redress the balance of our greed and selfishness, and act as channels for your transforming love.
All	**Lord, hear our prayer.**
	Amen.

The word

Reading

Reader	When the day of Pentecost had come, they were all together in one place. And suddenly from heaven there came a sound like the rush of a violent wind, and it filled the entire house where they were sitting. Divided tongues, as of fire, appeared among them, and a tongue rested on each of them. All of them were filled with the Holy Spirit and began to speak in other languages, as the Spirit gave them ability.

Now there were devout Jews from every nation under heaven living in Jerusalem. And at this sound the crowd gathered and was bewildered, because each one heard them speaking in the native language of each. Amazed and astonished, they asked, 'Are not all these who are speaking Galileans? And how is it that we hear, each of us, in our own native language? Parthians, Medes, Elamites, and residents of Mesopotamia, Judea and Cappadocia, Pontus and Asia, Phrygia and Pamphylia, Egypt and the parts of Libya belonging to Cyrene, and visitors from Rome, both Jews and proselytes, Cretans and Arabs – in our own languages we hear them speaking about God's deeds of power.' All were amazed and perplexed, saying to one another, 'What does this mean?' But others sneered and said, 'They are filled with new wine.'

But Peter, standing with the eleven, raised his voice and addressed them: 'Men of Judea and all who live in Jerusalem, let this be known to you, and listen to what I say. Indeed, these are not drunk, as you suppose, for it is only nine o'clock in the morning. No, this is what was spoken through the prophet Joel:

'In the last days it will be, God declares,

that I will pour out my Spirit upon all flesh,
and your sons and your daughters shall prophesy,
and your young men shall see visions,
and your old men shall dream dreams.
Even upon my slaves, both men and women,
in those days I will pour out my Spirit;
and they shall prophesy.
And I will show portents in the heaven above
and signs on the earth below,
blood, and fire, and smoky mist.
The sun shall be turned to darkness
and the moon to blood,
before the coming of the Lord's great and glorious day.'

Acts 2.1–21

Song or hymn of invocation

Address, reflection or video showing Christian Aid's work

Silent reflection

Prayers of intercession

The Offering

Song or hymn of offering

Offering our actions and our gifts

Ask each person to take time to reflect and to think of some action they can take that will make a difference to the work of Christian Aid and to write it on their tongue of flame. Then invite people to come and pin their flame to a board to make a Pentecostal fire, symbolizing how in the power of the Holy Spirit our actions can make a difference.

Once all the flames have been attached to the board to make a symbolic fire, the following words are said:

Leader   Come, Holy Spirit, move in our hearts and inspire us now to respond to the needs of your world through our prayers, our giving and the offering of our words and actions.

Leader We are the voice that speaks up for those whose voices are not heard.

All **Many voices joining their unheard cries.**

Leader One voice speaking out the truth can change a community.

All **Many voices speaking out the truth in unity can change the world.**

Leader One person giving generously can change a life.

All **Many people giving sacrificially can change the world.**

Leader One person taking action can make a difference.

All **Many people acting together can transform the future.**

Leader One voice lifted up in prayer moves the Father's heart.

All **We are many voices, calling for justice, freedom and transformation.**

Leader We join our voices to the cries of those whose voices are not heard, and together we raise them to intercede for change in our world.

All **God of the rushing wind,**
sweep through my indifference.
God of the fiery flames,
ignite my compassion.
God of the many voices,
open my mouth to speak out against injustice
that through your Spirit
and my actions
this world may be transformed.
Amen.

Sending out

Commissioning prayer

Leader As we celebrate the coming of the Holy Spirit and the empowering of God's people, let us ask for God's Spirit to fill us as we respond to God's call to go out into the world to listen and work with those whose voices are not heard:

Ever-present God, we are your hands and feet on earth. Help us to go in peace and serve with love. Fill us with your Spirit that we may stand with people across the world seeking justice and peace, and bless us with your strength that together we may build your kingdom here on earth.

All Amen.

Song or hymn of sending out

Closing responses

Leader	In the face of poverty and injustice
All	**we will not give in.**
Leader	With communities around the world
All	**we will not give in.**
Leader	Empowered by the Spirit
All	**we will not give in.**
Leader	And so may the blessing of God,
	Life-giver, Change-maker, Love-creator,
	be with us now and always.
All	**Amen.**

IN THE POWER OF THE SPIRIT

Welcome and introduction

Opening hymn invoking the presence of the Holy Spirit

Candle lighting and prayer

During the lighting of the candle and the saying of the prayer, a quiet meditative chant may be sung in the background.

Leader	We light this candle in the name of God:
	The God who illuminates the world and inspires us with the breath of life;
	The Son who has come that all may have life in fullness;
	The Spirit who embraces the world and blesses our souls with love.
All	**Amen.**

Call to worship

Reader 1	In the beginning when God created the heavens and the earth, the earth was formless and void . . . Then God said: 'let there by light'. And there was light.

Genesis 1.1

All   **And God was the light and it was good.**

Leader   O God, for your love for us, warm and brooding, which has brought us to birth and opened our eyes to the wonder of your creation,

All   **we give you thanks.**

Leader   For your love for us, wild and freeing, which has awakened us to the energy of creation: to the sap that flows, the blood that pulses, the heart that sings,

All   **we give you thanks.**

Leader   For your love for us, compassionate and patient, which has carried us through our pain, wept beside us in our sin and waited with us in our confusion,

All   **we give you thanks.**

Leader   For your love for us, strong and challenging, which has called us to risk for you, asked for the best in us, and shown us how to serve,

All   **we give you thanks.**

Leader   For your Holy Spirit present deep within us, and at the heart of all life,

All   **we give you thanks.**

Reader 2   Then God said, 'Let us make humankind in our own image, according to our likeness . . .' So God created humankind in God's own image, in the image of God, God created them. Male and female, God created them . . .

Genesis 1.26–27

All   **And God blessed them.**

Reader 3   And God saw everything that God had made, and indeed it was very good.

Genesis 1.31

Reader 4   I have come that they may have life and have it to the full.

John 10.10

All   **We give you thanks.**

Exploring God's word

Before the address, allow time for listening to music, played or recorded, that is both reflective and life-giving, encouraging listeners to be open and receptive to what they hear and to one another.

Address or reflection

Agape meal

Leader   An *Agape* is not a formal sacramental communion. It is a symbolic sharing of God's love – his *agape* – and of our care for one another, through the sharing of the bread and the wine by which we bless each other. All are invited to participate because Christ's invitation is inclusive.

Leader   O risen Christ, you made yourself known to the disciples
in the breaking of bread to the 5,000.
The bread which we now break together
is a sign of the brokenness of the world.
Through our sharing in the bread of life
in our many Christian communities,
and through the power of your Spirit,
open our eyes and hands to the needs of all people.

As your yourself drank from the cup
and shared it with your friends,
we drink this wine as we share our hope
that another world is possible,
where all can enjoy the promise of the fullness of life.

Let our hearts burn to share your gifts
and help us to go forth in the power of the Spirit
remembering our fellowship
as the one body, the diverse Body of Christ,
symbolized by this sharing of the bread:
bread of hope, bread of life, bread of peace. Amen.

As we share in this small love feast, let us pause as we give
each other the bread and the cup, and remind each other of
the blessing in it:

As the bread and cup is passed from one person to the next, each person says:

>The bread of fellowship, (or hope, or peace or life)
>The cup of life (or hope, or peace or life)

During the sharing of the bread and the cup, background music can be played or sung.

Prayer of commitment

Leader Spirit of unity, we pray for your Church.
Fill your people with all unity and peace.
Where we are corrupt, purify us.
Where we are in error, direct us.
Where anything in us is amiss, reform us.
Where we are right, strengthen us.
Where we are in need, provide for us.
Where we are divided, reunite us.

All **Gracious and loving God,**
We give you thanks
for uniting us in baptism in the body of Christ.
Guide us to towards the unity of your Church
and help us to treasure all things of reconciliation
that we may be led towards fullness of life,
through Jesus Christ, your Son, our Lord,
who lives and reigns with you
in the unity of the Holy Spirit,
ever one God, world without end. Amen.

Closing hymn celebrating fellowship

Blessing and sending out

LOCK IN!

This service explores what it means to be free and the nature of God's freedom in the Spirit.

Preparation

You will need an empty picture frame, or equivalent, filled with plasticine or playdough, in which impressions of keys can be made.

The Approach

Opening prayer

Leader   Loving God,
open our hearts,
so that we may feel your presence here among us.
Unclench our hands,
so that we may reach out and touch others.
Open our lips,
that we might sing your praise and announce your truth.
Unclog our ears,
to hear your agony in our inhumanity.
Open our eyes,
that we might see Christ in friend and foe alike.
Breathe your spirit on us this morning,
that we may know Christ among us.
Amen

Opening song

Reflection

Leader   How many of you possess a set of keys? Most of us have at least one – a house key, a car key, a locker key, perhaps.

How many of you possess a set of keys? Most of us have at least one – a house key, a car key, a locker key, perhaps.

If you've got some keys, take them out and hold them. Take a few moments and think about what they say about you and your life. What are all your keys for? Does each one signify a possession? Do any of them have a story?

Silence

> Keys are for security. They lock things up and keep them safe. They also lock up law-breakers and keep society safe. But keys are also used to oppress – to lock up dissidents and protesters, for example.

Silence

> For some, keys are about safety and security. They are symbols of freedom. For others, keys are about oppression and injustice. They are symbols of imprisonment.

Silence

Song invoking stillness and silence

Confession and absolution

Leader   If we have enjoyed our freedom to worship you, but failed to ask why others do not enjoy the same freedom,

All   **Lord, forgive us.**

Leader   If we have praised your for your unfailing generosity, yet locked away our possessions where no one else can share them,

All   **Lord, forgive us.**

Leader   If we have valued our own freedom so highly that others have been forced to pay with theirs,

All   **Lord, forgive us.**

Leader   If we have preached your word, yet forgotten the prisoner and ignored the needs of the sick or hungry,

All   **Lord, forgive us.**

Silence

Leader   The God of all freedom forgives us and frees us from the bondage of the sin that oppresses us that we may walk freely to love others as he loves us. Amen.

The Word

A story from Haiti

Leader Having thought about how keys can speak to us of freedom and oppression, let us listen to a story from Haiti about both of these things and the ultimate triumph of forgiveness, courage and compassion.

Reader 1 The National Coalition for Haitian Rights – that's NCHR for short – is a former Christian Aid partner that defends the rights of prisoners in Haiti.

Reader 2 There are 3,570 prisoners across 19 prisons in Haiti.

Reader 1 NCHR works to rehabilitate prisoners. It tells them about their rights and responsibilities and provides them with medical supplies. Most importantly, it campaigns for the courts to take up their cases.

Reader 2 Many wait for years before their case is heard. Imagine – 80 per cent of those held have not been tried or sentenced, which means massive overcrowding and the rapid spread of illness and epidemics within the prisons.

Reader 1 Marie Yolene Gilles works for NCHR but was a journalist before she was forced to flee the country for fear of her life. In the late 1980s, she was attacked by troops of President Prosper Avril for speaking out against the oppressive regime and human rights' abuses. Her colleagues were killed and the radio station where they worked was wrecked.

Reader 2 When the situation in Haiti changed, she returned and began working with NCHR, defending the rights of prisoners. She and her family are under constant threat of their lives.

Reader 1 But Marie is committed to the pursuit of justice, including defending the rights of all prisoners, even those who have oppressed the rights of others. 'It is my choice. I am not saying it is easy, but it is my choice,' she says.

Reader 2 She is now responsible for defending the rights of a prisoner accused of murder and of plotting against the state. The prisoner is Prosper Avril – the former President who tried to secure her death.

Reader 1   I was in prison and you visited me.

The Response

Free prayer

*There follows a time for free prayer in which prayers for prisoners,
those whose freedom is curtailed and those who work for human rights
can be offered. After each prayer the following response may be used:*

>   Lord, in your mercy,
>   **bring freedom, bring peace.**

The biddings may be brought to a close with the following prayer:

Leader   We ask all these things in the name of our liberator, Jesus
Christ, who for our sake was imprisoned, tried and con-
victed that we might be released from our sins and so know
perfect freedom. Amen.

Making a key collage

*The plasticine picture frame should be placed somewhere visible and
accessible.*
   *Invite everyone to come and make an impression of one or more
of their keys in the plasticine in whatever way they want – higgledy
piggledy, overlapping or upside down.*

Leader   As we sing a song of liberation, please come up to the front
with a key and press it into the plasticine. The end collage
will be a symbol of our safety and security as well as being
an expression of our artistic freedom. More importantly, it
will be a reminder to us of those whose freedom is curtailed,
either through poverty, imprisonment or conflict.

Song of liberation

Closing reflection

Reader   We say this must change
but nothing will change
until the poorest and weakest
know their own strength

Nothing will change
until the poorest person realizes
they are a human being
as good as other human beings

Nothing will change
until we understand that
we are children of God
we are full of freedoms
that come from God.

From Haiti

Closing song

Prayer of commitment

All   I chose to go from this place
determined to use my freedom
to help those without.
Determined to use my possessions
to share with those without.
Determined to use to my time
to pray for those with time on their hands.

Holy Spirit of God,
ignite your flame within me
and keep it burning.
Amen.

Creation and Harvest

In many parts of the world, churches celebrate 'Creation Day' on 1 September. They also set the period from this day to 4 October (the feast day of St Francis of Assisi) or the Sunday after 4 October as 'Creation Time'. It is around this time that many churches in our own country hold their harvest festivals, celebrating the fruits of God's earth and traditionally giving thanks for the safe gathering in of the harvest.

Whether one is celebrating Creation Day or Harvest Festival, these two festivals provide an opportunity for the Church to celebrate creation and to reflect on our roles as stewards of God's creation. Being made in the image of God means we are called to be co-creators, rejoicing and nurturing the diversity of God's earth rather than plundering its resources.

As the gentle balance of nature is disturbed by global warming, our need to treasure the earth rather than exploit its treasures gets ever more urgent. And as the effects of climate change are felt, our need to love our global neighbour takes on a new significance because the poorest of the earth are the most vulnerable. With this in mind, the liturgies in this section are designed both to celebrate God's creation and to challenge our response to it.

A SERVICE OF THANKSGIVING

This service is about thanksgiving: giving thanks for all the good things God provides and celebrating the good things we share. It focuses not only on the gifts of God's creation but also the gifts we can offer God in the service of others.

The Approach

The start of the service is announced with the beating of a drum or another clear symbol.

Call to worship

Leader	Make a joyful noise to the Lord, all the earth,
All	**worship the Lord with gladness,**
	come into the presence with singing!

Leader	We come together as the Family of God
All	**to offer praise and thanksgiving to our Lord,**
	to experience the living Word
	and to seek for ourselves and others
	the presence, direction, and power of the Holy Spirit.
	So be it!

Hymn or song

Prayer

All	**Almighty God, Creator and Sustainer of all,**
	we praise and thank you for your grace revealed in creation:

Leader	Your glory in the sun, moon and myriad stars,
	your might and majesty in mountain peaks and deep-set gorges,
	your power in the roaring of the never-resting oceans,
	your creativity in the mighty rhino and the minuscule moth,
	your life in the forests and lakes that give life abundantly,
	your mystery in the stark beauty of desert and field.
All	**We praise and adore you – you alone are our God!**
	Eternal Saviour, our Lord Jesus Christ,
	we praise and thank you for your love revealed on the cross:

Leader	In your miraculous birth we see God reaching into our world,
	in your life we see our full potential in love,
	in your arrest and trial we are confronted with our own turmoil and troubles,
	in your death we too are dead to sin, its power and its potential,
	in your resurrection we are raised from eternal death to eternal life,
	in your final return we see the future of our hopes and our world.

All   We praise and adore you – you alone are our God!
Holy Spirit, giver of comfort and life,
we praise and thank you for the life we live with you within:

Leader   For revealing in us that which is not of God,
for revealing Jesus in our lives as we live with you,
for comfort and guidance in our time of need,
for empowering us to live as the Church in love and
        wholeness,
for giving each one of us gifts as you desire that we may
        serve you and one another,
for filling our lives with love that we may transform our
        world.

All   We praise and adore you – you alone are our God!

Song of praise

Confession

Leader   Lord God
– gracious parent, loving Saviour and ever-present Spirit –
as we think of your majesty, grace, truth and love,
we are aware that much of our life does not reflect you.
Striving to live in your light,
the shadow within each continues to haunt us.
Let us, in silence, reflect on how we have responded to the
presence, promises and call of God in our lives.

Silence

Leader   Let us confess our sins to Almighty God.

All   Lord God,
we bow before you in penitence and pain.
Living on your earth, we desecrate and destroy creation.
Serving you, we so often choose to live our own way.
Experiencing your grace, we hate and hurt each other.
Knowing your truth, we so easily lie and create scandal.
Living in your love, we ignore those you died to save.
Lord God,
loving parent, eternal Saviour, and empowering Spirit,
we humbly ask you to forgive our sins:

for not loving you as we are set free to love,
for not loving all those you love,
for not loving ourselves.
Cleanse us, we pray.
Fill us with love anew
and empower us to love as you love us.

Leader   As the family of God – children of the Creator,
brothers and sisters of Jesus, one in the Spirit –
we hear the words of divine grace:
'Your sins are forgiven, be at peace!'
All   **We praise and adore you – you alone are our God!**

Song of thanksgiving

During the song, offerings are made, for example, fruits of the earth, money, pledges of time and talents, things children have made, drawn or painted.

The Offering is received, and thanks given:

Leader   Lord God –
gracious parent, eternal light, and Christ-sent comforter –
All   **we thank and praise you for your love in our lives!**
Leader   We bring to you these our tithes and our offerings:
All   **in offering them we offer you our lives,**
to live and love in thanksgiving,
and to bring your kingdom into being.
So be it!

The Word

The reading

Hymn or song

Address or reflection

The Response

The prayers

The prayers make provision for naming our particular concerns.

Leader Lord God, loving creator and parent, we give thanks for this beautiful world that you have created and all those who live on it . . .

All **May we daily fulfil your command to care for our planet and for all who shares its life.**

Leader We give thanks for all your good gifts to us, for the fruits of the earth, our time and our talents . . .

All **May we rejoice in them and use them for the good of all, that your kingdom come on earth.**

Leader We bring to you all your children, especially those who cannot rejoice in their own lives . . .

All **May we reach out to them in love and grace, that they may grow towards fullness of life.**

Leader We bring to you all those who feel lost and who find comfort in temporary pleasures . . .

All **May we so live our lives in you that they may experience your love through us.**

Leader We bring to you those who are sad, sick or hungry, those whose lives are diminished through depression, unemployment, or homelessness . . .

All **May we be set free to reach out in love, that they may be strengthened in their need and comforted in their sorrow.**

Leader We bring to you our own needs, hopes and fears . . .

All **May we so know our need of you that we are ever strengthened to seek your will.**

Leader We bring you all these, our prayers,
in the name of the one who is the Light of the World,
and through whom we are restored,
our Lord Jesus Christ,
who taught us to pray together, saying:

Our Father . . .

Dismissal

Hymn or song

The blessing

All   May the amazing grace of our Lord Jesus Christ,
             the extravagant love of God,
             and the intimate friendship of the Holy Spirit,
             be with us all.
             So be it!

The service is drawn to a close with the beating of a drum, or with the congregation leaving in joyous song.

TAKE TIME . . .

This liturgy takes time as its theme, exploring the rhythms of life around the globe. It highlights our connectedness one with another and challenges us to manage our time and resources in a way that allows everyone to have a share in the harvest.

Preparation

You will need scatter cards with the following phrase written on one side:

For the world, it is a time to . . . .

And on the reverse, one of the following phrases from the book of Ecclesiastes:

A time to be born	A time to die
A time to plant	A time to uproot
A time to kill	A time to heal
A time to tear down	A time to build
A time to weep	A time to laugh
A time to mourn	A time to dance
A time to scatter stones	A time to gather stones
A time to embrace	A time to refrain from embracing
A time to search	A time to give up things

A time to keep	A time to throw away
A time to tear	A time to sew
A time to love	A time to hate
A time for war	A time for peace

Scatter the cards around the worship area, making sure that the above phrases are the right side up.

Ensure that there are a few spare blank cards available to fill in, and some pencils.

Welcome

Welcome those present and explain that the service is about time. Invite everyone to take their watches off, to put them in their pockets and spend the service in a timeless space.

Gathering song

Meditation

Leader   God of all times and seasons:
I come to you, the God of Spring – the new leaf God, the new life God – rejoicing in your creativity;
I come to you, the God of Summer – the colour God, the growing God – rejoicing in your sustenance;
I come to you, the God of Autumn – the harvest God, the richness God – rejoicing in your fruitfulness;
I come to you, the God of Winter – the waiting God, the still and secret God – rejoicing in your mystery;
And so, Creator, lead my time to the edge of your eternity,
gather my seasons into the shelter of your timelessness,
and there, in stillness and silence,
let me adore you.

Silence

Song

Reading

Reader   For everything there is a season, and a time for every
matter under heaven:

a time to be born, and a time to die;

a time to plant, and a time to pluck up what is planted;

a time to kill, and a time to heal;

a time to break down, and a time to build up;

a time to weep, and a time to laugh;

a time to mourn, and a time to dance;

a time to throw away stones, and a time to gather stones
together;

a time to embrace, and a time to refrain from embracing;

a time to seek, and a time to lose;

a time to keep, and a time to throw away;

a time to tear, and a time to sew;

a time to keep silence, and a time to speak;

a time to love, and a time to hate;

a time for war, and a time for peace.

What gain have the workers from their toil? I have seen the business that God has given to everyone to be busy with. He has made everything suitable for its time; moreover, he has put a sense of past and future into their minds, yet they cannot find out what God has done from the beginning to the end. I know that there is nothing better for them than to be happy and enjoy themselves as long as they live; moreover, it is God's gift that all should eat and drink and take pleasure in all their toil. I know that whatever God does endures for ever; nothing can be added to it, nor anything taken from it; God has done this, so that all should stand in awe before him.

Ecclesiastes 3.1–14

Taking time

Leader   What's the time? Not so easy to tell without a watch! But the more interesting thing to think about is 'what is the time for me right now? What's the season of my life?'

Invite people to choose a card that relates to their life at the moment and to keep it for the course of the service. Ask them to take their time to think carefully about which card they pick.

While people are moving around, play appropriate background music or invite a music group to sing quietly.

Reflection

Reader	The minutes of the hours belong to the Lord.
All	**The hours of the days are God's.**
Reader	The days of the years belong to the Lord.
All	**The years of my life are God's.**
Reader	We hold time tight in our hands.
All	**All our times are secure in God's hands.**
Reader	Take time to tell the God of all times and seasons why you chose the card. Pray for the right use of that time, for the Creator 'has made everything beautiful in its time'. And ask that God will fulfil his purpose in you through this stage of your life.

Silence

Leader	That everyone may eat and drink, and find satisfaction in all their toil – this is the gift of God.

Song

Reading

Reader	Moreover, it is God's gift that all should eat and drink and take pleasure in all their toil. I know that whatever God does endures for ever; nothing can be added to it, nor anything taken from it; God has done this, so that all should stand in awe before him. That which is, already has been; that which is to be, already is; and God seeks out what has gone by.
	Moreover, I saw under the sun that in the place of justice, wickedness was there, and in the place of righteousness, wickedness was there as well. I said in my heart, God will judge the righteous and the wicked.

Ecclesiastes 3.13–17 (with deliberate overlap with first reading)

A time tour of the world

Reader 1 In Mali it is coming up to 10.30 in the morning. The changing climate and the lack of rainfall means that Alimatou Kene, aged 55, will struggle to feed her nine children today and every day. The river that runs through Yawakanda – Alimatou's village – used to dry up in March, five months after the rainy season ended. It is now drying up in December or January, two or three months early. Inevitably this is having an impact on the villagers' ability to grow enough food. Christian Aid partner, APH, secured land near the river for 63 women to begin farming onions. Since Alimatou began growing onions on this land she has been able to earn enough money to feed her family three times a day. She can also clothe her entire family, buy medicines when they are sick, and she can afford to send her grandchildren to school.

'There is a time for every purpose under heaven.' What time is it for Alimatou?

Reader 2 In Burma it is three o'clock in the afternoon. Lwe May should live there, but she is in a refugee camp on the border of Thailand, taking refuge from the repressive military regime which has driven thousands from their homes. She and her husband and elder son had to leave when the army came looking for recruits, but they had to leave behind their daughter and six-year-old boy. Christian Aid's partner the Thailand–Burma Border Consortium provides food, mosquito nets and some building materials in the camps.

'There is a time for every purpose under heaven.' What time is it for Lwe May?

Reader 3 In the Dominican Republic it is half past four in the morning. Romero Esperanza is probably asleep in his dirt-floored, cardboard-walled room. But night time is not always safe on the sugar cane plantations. The army chooses the nights for raids against undocumented migrants from Haiti who work there as day labourers to send money back home to their families. The soldiers usually demand money or a bottle of rum – the alternative is to be handcuffed and thrown into the back of a truck. Christian Aids's programme in the Dominican Republic seeks to empower the poorest and most marginalized people into seeking justice.

'There is a time for every purpose under heaven.' What time is it for Romero?

Prayer time

Intercessions

Leader	Wherever it is time to eat, but food is scarce or poor, God of all justice and mercy,
All	**let this be a time of change.**

Leader	Wherever it is time to drink, but the water is dirty or diseased, God of all justice and mercy,
All	**let this be a time of change.**

Leader	Wherever it is time to work, but the labour is done for a pitiful reward, God of all justice and mercy,
All	**let this be a time of change.**

Leader	Wherever it is time to seek help, but the doctors are far and the medicines few, God of all justice and mercy,
All	**let this be a time of change.**

Leader	Wherever it is time for market, but the traders are forced into unfair deals, God of all justice and mercy,
All	**let this be a time of change.**

Leader	Wherever it is time for peace, but the killing continues and the people live in fear, God of all justice and mercy,
All	**let this be a time of change.**

Naming our prayer

Everyone is invited to turn their card over. As a resolution to take away and keep, people write in the gap what is their hope / prayer / vision for the world at this point. While they are writing or thinking, meditative music can be played or sung.

Leader   Thus says the LORD: In the time of favour I have answered you, on a day of salvation I have helped you; I have kept you and given you as a covenant to the people, to establish the land, to apportion the desolate heritages; saying to the prisoners, 'Come out,' to those who are in darkness, 'Show yourselves.' . . . Lo, these shall come from afar, and lo, these from the north and from the west.' . . . Sing for joy, O heavens, and exult, O earth; break forth O mountains, into singing! For the LORD has comforted his people, and will have compassion on his suffering ones.

Isaiah 49.8–9, 12–13

All   I tell you, now is the time of God's favour, now is the day of salvation. Now is the time to celebrate God's generous provision. Now is the time to harvest our time and our talents and to share them for the good of all.

Song

At this point, everyone is invited to guess how much time they have spent in this service and to retrieve their watches from their pockets, secure in the knowledge that God is the God of all time and that our times and seasons are safe with him through all eternity.

Closing declaration

All   All the past we leave behind,
And we take up the task eternal,
And the burden, and the lesson,
Conquering,
holding,
daring,
venturing,
So we go the unknown ways –
Pioneers, O pioneers!

From 'Pioneers, O pioneers!' by Walt Whitman

CELEBRATING CREATION

This service celebrates creation and challenges us to prioritize our lives so that we treasure the earth and our relationships over and above material wealth and possessions.

Preparation

You will need:

✠ a wooden cross
✠ a piece of paper and pencil for each person
✠ a large stone
✠ flowers – one for each person.

The Approach

Opening hymn or song

Reading

Reader   **The Summer Day**

Who made the world?
Who made the swan, and the black bear?
Who made the grasshopper?
This grasshopper, I mean –
the one who has flung herself out of the grass,
the one who is eating sugar out of my hand,
who is moving her jaws back and forth instead of up and
    down –
who is gazing around with her enormous and complicated
    eyes.
Now she lifts her pale forearms and thoroughly washes her
    face.
Now she snaps her wings open, and floats away.
I don't know exactly what a prayer is.
I do know how to pay attention, how to fall down
into the grass, how to kneel down in the grass,
how to be idle and blessed, how to stroll through the fields,
which is what I have been doing all day.
Tell me, what else should I have done?

Doesn't everything die at last, and too soon?
Tell me, what is it you plan to do
with your one wild and precious life?

Mary Oliver

Gathering song

Prayer of approach

Leader   Creator of the galaxies,
            ruler of the uttermost reaches of space,
            you are nearer to us than hands and feet,
            closer to us than our next breath.

            We sense your Presence
            in the tightly curled rose bud
            and in the open arms of a golden beach.
            We hear you in the sound of wind and waves
            and in the soft chatter of happy children.
            Your Presence is woven into the life of the world
            and into our lives
            and we are glad to sing your praise.

From 'The Green heart of the snowdrop', Kate McIlhagga

Litany of praise

Reader   In the beginning God made the world:
Women   **made it and mothered it,**
Men   **shaped it and fathered it.**
Reader   Filled it with seeds and with signs of fertility,
All   **filled it with love and its folk with ability.**

Reader   All that is green, blue, deep and growing:
All   **God's is the hand that created you.**

Reader   All that is tender, firm, fragrant and curious:
All   **God's is the hand that created you.**

Reader   All that crawls, flies, swims, walks or is motionless:
All   **God's is the hand that created you.**

Reader   All that screeches, sings, laughs, roars or is silent:
All   **God's is the hand that created you.**

Reader   All that suffers, lacks, groans or longs for an end:
All   **God's is the hand that created you.**

The world belongs to God,
The earth and all creation.

                A Wee Worship Book, *Wild Goose Worship Group*

Hymn or song

The Word

Leader   As we give thanks for the fruits of the earth, let us reflect on our calling to preserve God's creation, to live in holiness and to build a kingdom of justice and peace.

          Let us listen to the story of the rich young man from Mark's Gospel and allow its words to lead us into a time of guided meditation. Each period of silence will last for a few minutes and will be ended by a chant or a prayer.

Short period of silence

Reading Mark 10.17–27

Chant

Voice 1   Scientists are telling us that we are on the brink of a climate crisis. This is a crisis that will only be averted if we ask the question that this young man asked Jesus . . . what must we do? What must we do in order to reverse the tide of disaster for those already living with the effects of climate change and to leave an inheritance of life for those who come after us? How are we to deal with our addiction to consumption and our carbon-hungry lifestyles?

          The encounter of the rich young man with Jesus was a pivotal moment, a time for him to be challenged to re-evaluate his priorities and his attitude to God and his fellow human beings. Jesus cut straight to the heart of the issue and straight to his heart – you have to give up that which keeps you from doing what you really need to do.

Voice 2   The young man was a respectable, law-abiding devout Jew. He kept the commandments and did nothing to harm those around him. And yet he was ill-at-ease. First-century Palestine was a time of particular expectation among the Jews: a watershed between the present age and the age to come, the time of God's anticipated kingdom. He was wealthy, and at that time in Jewish culture, wealth was seen as evidence of God's blessing.

Voice 3   Spend a moment in silence thinking about what society encourages us to take for granted as blessing; perhaps the foreign holidays, our freedom of choice or the exciting pace of our lives.

Chant

Voice 3   We yearn to heal the damage to the world our actions have
        caused,
    yet we are afraid of the changes needed and wish to guard
        our lifestyles.
    We are divided within our souls and need God's healing.
    Let us confess our sins:

All   **For unrestrained economic growth,**
    for conspicuous consumption,
    for always wanting more,
    for not thinking through the consequences,
    for not caring for future generations,
    for blind indifference,
    forgive us our failing.

Silence

Voice 3   The forgiveness of the Maker, who knows us, be ours;
    the forgiveness of the Son, who knows life's struggles, be
       ours;
    the forgiveness of the Spirit, who encourages, be ours;
    the love of God, who enables life-giving change,
    be ours today and always.

All   **Creator God,**
Redeemer Son,
Guiding Spirit,
As forgiven people,
Help us to walk with a new lightness of step
And give us the resolve to touch the earth lightly in our
living in your world. Amen.

Andrew de Smet and Chris Polhill

Voice 4   Jesus had compassion on the young man and desperately
wanted to lead him to the answer to his question. Jesus
discerned his heart and what it was that was holding him
back from the full life of God's kingdom. The disciples were
clearly as shocked as the young man by the interchange
between him and Jesus. They, too, had bought into the idea
that wealth was a sign of God's favour. So Jesus shocks them
into a new understanding with a laughable statement: 'It is
easier for a camel to pass through the eye of a needle than
for someone who is rich to enter the kingdom of God.'

Jesus in this story is offering a gate, a way through from
one life to another.

He tells the young man, 'You lack one thing, go, sell what
you own and give the money to the poor and you will have
treasure in heaven; then come follow me.' In what Jesus
says, the young man glimpses what is on the other side of
that gate, but goes away shocked and grieving.

Voice 5   Today we are focusing on the climate crisis. So if we want to
pray about the future of the planet and our role in its care,
we might ask, as the young man did, what must we do? Not
to inherit eternal life, but to allow people a full and dignified
life in the here and now, and to leave an inheritance of life
for those who come after us.

What would we hear Jesus saying in reply?

Is there one thing we lack – the thing Jesus might ask us to
get rid of or change?

What is it that is destroying our relationship with the
earth and its people and thus, our relationship with God?

Are there things that get in the way of our relationship
with God and his creation – the so-called 'must haves' of
our lives? Our compliance with our consumer culture, our

energy-thirsty appliances or lifestyle? Our investment in financial security?

What must we shed? Let go of? Give away, in order that we might stand, open-armed and open-hearted, in the gateway – get a better glimpse of what is on the other side – and move forward?

Let us now spend a moment reflecting on this.

Silence

Chant

Voice 4   When Jesus says that it is very difficult for the rich to get into the kingdom of God, he's not talking about somewhere we go when we die, but somewhere that it open to us now. This is counter-cultural – Jesus invites us into the fullness of life in a culture where the meek shall inherit the earth and the merciful are blessed. Happy, he says, are the poor in spirit, are those who hunger and thirst for righteousness, are those who mourn. This is a culture clash – in head-on collision with our culture – that says 'happy are those who can buy cheap flights; happy are those who shop; blessed are the ones who live in big houses.' On the one hand, then, is the kingdom of God, the realm in which the power of God is pervasive and the values and priorities of God prevail; on the other, is a realm where other values and priorities prevail and the power of possessions and self-interest is what matters. And we, not surprisingly, find it a struggle to live in both at the same time.

Voice 5   Jesus teaches clearly that to pass through the eye of the needle, we need to be embracing the things of the kingdom of God. In giving something up, we are invited to take something up. Instead of feeling helpless in the face of climate crisis, we are invited to respond to the questions Jesus raises. How do we value our possessions? How do we value our neighbour? What kind of community do we want to build, locally and globally?

Let us spend a moment considering where, in the climate crisis, we might find new life. How might we do things differently? We might like to focus on how to share your resources creatively . . . is there potential here for friendship with our immediate neighbours? Or what we might do with the extra time we have if we were forced to slow down? Or whether we would actually be worse off taking the train rather than a plane to do a short journey?

Silence

Chant

Voice 4   How can we maintain a lifestyle that so disproportionately benefits us against others, and think that we are conforming to the values of God's kingdom, God's way of doing things? It is like trying to force ourselves through the needle's eye.

Voice 5   But we needn't feel overwhelmed. God gives us choices and we have the opportunity to model a different way of living. Spend a moment sharing with your immediate neighbour where you sense a lifestyle change that you could make.

Hymn or song

Voice 4   Let's be clear. The opposite of obsessive and exploitative wealth is not poverty. Poverty crushes hope and denies potential, it undermines our humanity by making the fight for survival our dominating aim. It humiliates us, it prevents us from taking control of our own lives. Poverty is most certainly not God's will for us; it has no place in God's culture. Poverty, like wealth, is a physical and spiritual problem.

Voice 1   God's kingdom is a challenge to our values, our culture and the way we see the world. It challenges us to see that our material wealth and others' material poverty are both spiritual diseases. Poor communities are directly suffering as a result of our lifestyles. But we can engage in healing. By supporting development projects, as well as making lifestyle changes and lobbying governments, we are taking action so that together we may become spiritually rich and wholly sustained.

The Response

Voice 4   The message of the gospel is challenging but at the same time it is constant and encouraging. Jesus, who encourages neither poverty nor riches, is clear, though exasperatingly elusive. When the disciples were astounded and ask each other, 'Who can be saved?', Jesus looks at them and says, 'For mortals, it is impossible, but not for God; for God all things are possible.' The things of the world can entangle and constrain us. Yet it is always possible, by the grace of God, to cut loose and enter into the freedom that Jesus inhabited, his disciples shared and which is the lived experience of the kingdom and rule of God: a kingdom beyond the domain of possessions and riches but where all know the worth of community and relationship.

Voice 5   Let us take some time now to consider where God is inviting us into new life.
What is it we think that Christ is asking us to let go of/set aside?
In the stillness, let us listen to our hearts . . .

Pause

To offer this in prayer, we may think of putting a word or a phrase or an image onto the piece of paper we have, to represent what we need to lay down.

Pause

As the song begins, we may wish to place this under a stone around the cross, as a symbol of the burdens that block our relationship with God. As we lay these down, let us take a flower as a symbol of the new life that we are offered by Christ.

Sending out

Closing responses

Leader   Through Christ, the first born of all creation,
All   we pray for respect for the earth.

Leader	Through Christ, prince of peace,
All	**we pray for peace for the earth's peoples.**
Leader	Through Christ, King of love,
All	**we pray for love in our lives.**
Leader	Through Christ lord of the dance,
All	**we pray for delight in the good.**
Leader	Through Christ, morning star, rising over our world,
All	**we pray for the grace to make a new start for ourselves and for the world.**
Leader	And may God bless us and keep us, today and each day,
All	**the Father, the Son and the Holy Spirit,**
Leader	and until we meet again
All	**may God hold us in the palm of his hand. Amen.**

Closing hymn or song

NOT CARBON NEUTRAL

This service both celebrates God's amazing world and everything in it, and challenges us to look at our lifestyles which are damaging the world's climate. The way we have set up the world to work in our favour – our factories, our cheap flights, our reliance on fossil fuels – means we are producing too much carbon dioxide, which causes global warming. Our global neighbours bear the brunt. Knowing we are involved means we cannot be neutral.

Preparation

You will need a supply of charcoal for marking foreheads or the backs of hands during the service. Decide how this will happen beforehand and have the charcoal ready to hand out.

The Gathering

Welcome and opening responses

Song of praise to the Creator

Celebrating creation

Leader 1   God has made an amazing world . . .
Cheetahs can run at 60 miles an hour.

Leader 2   Mother hens turn over their eggs 50 times a day.

Leader 1   There have been 6,000 lightning strikes somewhere in the world in the last minute.

Leader 2   All the ants in the world weigh more than all the people in the world.

Leader 1   There are 500 million tonnes of krill in the Southern Ocean.

Leader 2   Butterflies taste with their feet.

Leader 1   Chameleons can move their eyes to look in two different directions at the same time.

Leader 2   Many types of spider have eight eyes.

Leader 1   Male emperor penguins can survive at minus 50° Celsius.

Leader 2   One hectare of rainforest may contain 250 different species of trees.

Leader 1   God has made an amazing world.

We come before God who created this amazing world and everything in it, knowing that our actions and our lifestyles are damaging the world's climate; and it is not just plants and animals that are affected. We all are, but most particularly, our neighbours in the Global South are feeling the adverse effects of global warming. Knowing we are involved means we cannot be neutral.

Leader 2   The overwhelming scientific consensus is that increases in carbon dioxide in the atmosphere caused by human activity are responsible for climate change.

Leader 1   Because of climate change, 150 million people will become environmental refugees by 2050.

Leader 2   The amount of oil we burn in six weeks would have lasted for an entire year in the 1950s.

Leader 1   30 million more people will go hungry by 2050, because of
climate change reducing agricultural yields.

Leader 2   20 per cent of the world's population, living in industrial-
ized countries, consume 60 per cent of the world's commercial energy.

Leader 1   A rise of 2–3° Celsius, expected by 2050, will lead to water
scarcity for two billion people.

Leader 2   We use five times more fossil fuels than we did 20 years
ago.

Leader 1   By 2080, 75 per cent of Africa's population could be at risk
of hunger due to climate change.

The Approach

Prayer

Leader 1   Creator and sustainer of all life,
who has blessed us and brought us here this day,
we give you thanks for all that we have
and all that we are,
for without you, we are but nothing.

We come before you, Lord,
and we do not come alone.
With our brothers and sisters in Christ,
and with all creation,
we come to join the hymn of unending praise.

We come today as a minority;
we are rich people
from the developed world,
but we come mindful of the majority –
people who are poor and vulnerable living in the
developing world.

We come as the stewards of creation,
the consumers of the world's goodness
and the ones who unwittingly have helped to create climate
change.

Gracious and loving God,
meet us as we come to you today.
Hear us as we pray for understanding
and help us as we seek to change,
for the sake of your kingdom, Amen.

Song

Reading   Based on Matthew 25.

Reader 1   When the Son of Man comes in his glory with all of his angels, he will sit on his royal throne. The people of all nations will be brought before him, and he will separate them, as shepherds separate their sheep from their goats.

He will place the sheep on his right and the goats on his left. The king will say to those on his left, 'Get away from me! You are under God's curse. Go into the everlasting fire prepared for the devil and his angels!'

Reader 2   Thirty-five years ago Abdoulaye Diack in Senegal made his living cutting down trees to make charcoal. But cutting down trees allowed the desert to expand and in the end brought drought. In 1973, when drought hit the country, no one in his village was able to grow any food.

The desert is encroaching on the country at a rate of 300m a year. Traditional agriculture, using the predictable annual local flooding of rivers and nomadic cattle herding, has been so damaged over such a long period that it is never expected to support people as it did before.

Reader 1   I was hungry and you sent me a famine.

Short pause

Reader 2   Monica Wayua Kilini is 48 years old and is widowed with eight children. For the last four years, she has not been able to grow any food as the rains keep failing. Monica often relies on the generosity of her neighbours to provide food for her children, or they go searching for wild fruits. There is no clean water nearby, so every day Monica walks for four hours to collect water from a river.

Reader 1   I was thirsty and you caused the rains to fail.

Short pause

Reader 2   Twelve-year-old Champa from Bangladesh has lost her home three times and three times her family has got back on its feet and built a new life, only for the river to take everything again. Champa's apprehension is understandable. 'If we lose our house again, where will we go? I am frightened of the river.'

A rise in sea level of between 90–95cm by the year 2100 – towards the top end of scientific forecasts – could displace 35 million and leave about 18 per cent of the country permanently under water.

Reader 1   I was naked and you caused the waters to take away my home.

Short pause

Reader 2   And they said to him, 'When was it that we saw you hungry and sent you a famine, thirsty and caused the rains to fail, naked and caused the waters to take away your home?'

Reader 1   The king will answer, 'Whenever you did it for any of my people, no matter how unimportant they seemed, you did it for me.'

Time for silent reflection

Confession

Leader 2   During the singing of *Kyrie eleison*, which means 'Lord have mercy', as a sign of penitence, you are invited to mark each other with a cross using charcoal, either on the backs of our hands or our foreheads, in the way that many Christians sign themselves with ash on Ash Wednesday.

Today we use charcoal to remind ourselves of the story of Abdoulaye in Senegal and, because the carbon is a reminder of the carbon dioxide that is damaging this planet.

As we sign the cross, let us offer these words of forgiveness:

The God of all creation forgives us and blesses us.

Before we mark each other, let us pray:

All   **God of all creation,**
we dare to come to you in worship
with hands dirty from what we have done to your world,
with hearts heavy with the knowledge of how we have let
you down,
with minds reeling with facts and predictions of catastrophe.

Leader 1 Hear us now as we pray to you in penitence . . .

Chant   'Kyrie eleison' (Taizé) repeatedly

As the singing begins the charcoal is distributed. When everyone who wishes to has been marked, all join in these words of forgiveness:

All   **For what we have done in ignorance or carelessness,**
for what we have done, knowing it to be wrong,
for what we have done in arrogance or thoughtlessness,
God forgive us.

Leader 2 The God of all creation forgives us and blesses us.
All   **Thanks be to God.**

Words of hope

Leader 1 Let us choose to work and to pray for a better future. Let us choose to stand alongside those who are working to overcome drought, famine and disaster. Let us choose to celebrate with those who will not give up.

So let us pray:

As Christians we will live
not in despair, but in hope,
not in fear, but in determination,
not relying on our ingenuity

but trusting in you, our God –
the author, maker and redeemer of all things. Amen.

Song

Prayer

All   **God of all creation,
make our hearts restless.
Call us to act,
move us to give,
inspire us to pray.
May your love for all creation
fill us down to our toes.
Make our bodies restless
to do your will.
Amen.**

Reading Based on Matthew 25 (revisited).

Reader 1 When the Son of Man comes in his glory with all of his angels, he will sit on his royal throne. The people of all nations will be brought before him, and he will separate them, as shepherds separate their sheep from their goats.

He will place the sheep on his right and the goats on his left.

Then the king will say to those on his right, 'My father has blessed you! Come and receive the kingdom that was prepared for you before the world was created.'

Reader 2 Abdoulaye in Senegal is now one of a network of people planting trees in Senegal, in contrast to his previous livelihood based on cutting them down. Christian Aid worked with the *Union pour la Solidarité et l'Entraide* (USE), helping communities plant large numbers of trees, which give shade, provide fruit to eat and sell, and improve the environment and eco-system of their local area.

Reader 1 I was hungry and you gave me seeds to plant fruit trees.

Reader 2 Judith from Zimbabwe is a widow with five children. She used to have to fetch her family's drinking water from the nearby river. It wasn't clean and her children often fell sick. Now, with help from her neighbours and Christian Aid's partner, the Zimbabwe Council of Churches (ZCC) she's built a pipe and tank system to harvest and store rainwater. She and her children now have clean water, on tap, at home.

Reader 1   I was thirsty and you paid for my clean water supply.

Reader 2   The village of Nuevo Amanecer in Nicaragua has prepared itself for future emergencies. They have a community grain store and a unique system of detecting which houses are most at risk from heavy rains and hurricanes. They are colour coded on a community map, so people know whom to help first when climate disaster strikes

Reader1   I was naked and you cared for me.

Reader 2   And they said to him, 'When was it that we saw you hungry and gave you seeds, thirsty and paid for clean water, naked and cared for you?'

Reader 1   The king will answer, 'Whenever you did it for any of my people, no matter how unimportant they seemed, you did it for me.'

Song

Sending out

Blessing

Leader   May the God of all creation,
who can move worlds or uncurl a butterfly's wing,
help us to carry our questions, our doubts and our
   struggles

May the Son who came to live with us
show us how to be and act
so that God may be revealed.

And may the Spirit who broods over creation,
sustain us and stir us deeply,

so that through our living and our loving,
the most ordinary of places in the world
may be touched by heaven.
Amen.

BOYS AND GIRLS COME OUT TO PRAY

When we reflect on our relationship with God and creation it is easy to forget that our human relationships are part of the equation. To be in harmony with the created order we need to be in right relationship with our fellow human beings, to be at peace with ourselves and comfortable in our own skin.

How we see ourselves and how we see others is often bound up with issues surrounding gender. This service explores the gender relationship, issues of inequality and what it means to be made in the image of God.

Preparation

You will need:

✠ two large (2-metre high) mannequins of a naked man and woman to go at front of worship space
✠ postcards with holes punched in the corner, threaded with lengths of ribbon in stereotypical pink and blue
✠ pencils
✠ six readers: 1 to 4 should be women, 5 and 6 should be men.

Welcome

Song of praise to the Creator

Reading

Reader   Then God said, 'Let us make humankind in our image, according to our likeness; and let them have dominion over the fish of the sea, and over the birds of the air, and over the cattle, and over all the wild animals of the earth, and over every creeping thing that creeps upon the earth.'

        So God created humankind in his image, in the image of

God he created them; male and female he created them. God saw everything that he had made, and indeed, it was very good. And there was evening and there was morning, the sixth day.

Thus the heavens and the earth were finished, and all their multitude.

Genesis 1.26–27, 31; 2.1)

Introduction

Leader   'Male and female God created them – in the image of God they were created.' This comes from the story at the beginning of the Bible that explores the question of creation. In this service we also will explore that first heaven@earth encounter.

Notice how the very first reference to humans in the Bible puts male and female side by side – equal, complementary, both taking after God in character and in spirit.

So let us begin with the good news about being female and the good news about being male by listening to these two celebratory poems. This will be followed by some reflection time – time to think about what you enjoy about being your gender – and talk with God about it.

Poems

Leader   First of all a poem by Maya Angelou.

Reader 1   Pretty women wonder where my secret lies.
I'm not cute or built to suit a fashion model's size
But when I start to tell them,
They think I'm telling lies.
I say,
It's in the reach of my arms
The span of my hips,
The stride of my step,
The curl of my lips.
I'm a woman
Phenomenally.
Phenomenal woman, that's me.

Reader 2   I walk into a room
Just as cool as you please,
And to a man,
The fellows stand or
Fall down on their knees.
Then they swarm around me,
A hive of honey bees.
I say,
It's the fire in my eyes,
And the flash of my teeth,
The swing in my waist,
And the joy in my feet.
I'm a woman
Phenomenally.
Phenomenal woman, that's me.

Reader 3   Men themselves have wondered
What they see in me.
They try so much
But they can't touch
My inner mystery.
When I try to show them
They say they still can't see.
I say,
It's the arch of my back,
The sun of my smile,
The ride of my breasts,
The grace of my style.
I'm a woman
Phenomenally.
Phenomenal woman, that's me.

Reader 4   Now you understand
Just why my head's not bowed.
I don't shout or jump about
Or have to talk real loud.
When you see me passing
It ought to make you proud.
I say,
It's in the click of my heels,
The bend of my hair,
the palm of my hand,

The need of my care.
'Cause I'm a woman
Phenomenally.
Phenomenal woman, that's me.

From Phenomenal Woman: Four Poems Celebrating Women
by Maya Angelou

Leader And now Shakespeare is going in to bat for the men. This is from Hamlet:
What a piece of work is a man!

Reader 5 How noble in reason!

Reader 6 How infinite in faculty!

Reader 5 In form and moving how express and admirable!

Reader 6 In action how like an angel!

Reader 5 In apprehension how like a god!

Reader 6 The beauty of the world!

Reader 5 The paragon of animals!

Reader 6 This quintessence of all dust.

Reflection time

Reflective music is played or a singing group sing a reflective but positive song during which time people have the opportunity to think and pray.

Prayer

Leader We share the prayer of the 14th-century mystic Julian of Norwich.

All O God,
as truly as you are our father,
so just as truly are you our mother.
We thank you, God our father,
for your strength and goodness.
We thank you, God our mother,
for the closeness of your caring.
O God, we thank you for the great love

you have for each one of us.
Amen.

Reflection

Reader 4   As we think about the way men are, and the way women are, we can't help but realize that something has gone wrong. Whenever we hear the words 'Typical man!' or 'Typical woman!' it is never a compliment – it's always a put down. So why is that? Whatever has happened to the way gender roles have developed and are perceived cannot possibly have been the way God intended. It's hard to recognize the vision of men and women equal and complementary that begins the Bible when we look at the gender divide that is reality.

Reader 2   Sometimes Western society seems enlightened in the way it approaches gender.

Reader 3   Sometimes it seems to be creating more stereotypes than it addresses.

Reader 4   Lord, have mercy.

Reader 2   Sometimes the world seems to be making advances toward equality.

Reader 3   Sometimes we might as well be back in the caves.

Reader 4   Lord, have mercy.

Reader 2   Sometimes Christianity seems to be at the forefront of confronting attitudes that for centuries favoured men at the expense of women.

Reader 3   Sometimes it seems to be part of the problem.

Reader 4   Lord, have mercy.

Reader 2   Worldwide, women make up one-third of the work force.

Reader 3   They earn one tenth of the world's wages.

Reader 2   They are entitled to one tenth of the world's rights.

Reader 3   Of the people who live in absolute poverty – that's less than one dollar per day – four-fifths are women.

Reader 2   That's 900,000,000.

Reader 3 In the UK, there were 160,026 incidents of violence by men against women reported to the police during 1999.

Reader 2 An estimated 6,000 girls are subjected to circumcision – per day.

Reader 4 Lord, have mercy.
Christ, have mercy.
Lord, have mercy.

Reflective song of confession

Reading

Reader 1 This passage is taken from the account of the death of Jesus, after Pilate has surrendered him to the will of the crowd.

As they led him away, they seized a man, Simon of Cyrene, who was coming from the country, and they laid the cross on him, and made him carry it behind Jesus. A great number of the people followed him, and among them were women who were beating their breasts and wailing for him. But Jesus turned to them and said, 'Daughters of Jerusalem, do not weep for me, but weep for yourselves and for your children. For the days are surely coming when they will say, 'Blessed are the barren, and the wombs that never bore, and the breasts that never nursed.' Then they will begin to say to the mountains, 'Fall on us'; and to the hills, 'Cover us.' For if they do this when the wood is green, what will happen when it is dry?'

Luke 23.26–31

Prayer

Reader 2 For the women who are trapped by fear of men's physical strength or anger, a prayer.

Reader 3 Jesus says, 'Do not weep for me; weep for yourselves and for your children.'

All **Lord, we cry to you for peace.**

Reader 2 For the men who are hostage to the stereotypes and expectations of their culture, a prayer.

Reader 3   'Do not weep for me; weep for yourselves and for your children.'

All   **Lord, we cry to you for tolerance.**

Reader 2   For all whose bodies have been abused as a weapon of oppression, a prayer.

Reader 3   'Do not weep for me; weep for yourselves and for your children.'

All   **Lord, we cry to you for healing.**

Reader 2   For everyone whose gender has denied them dignity or value or basic human rights, a prayer.

Reader 3   'Do not weep for me; weep for yourselves and for your children.'

All   **Lord, we cry to you for justice.**

Bible reading

Reader 4   A reading from Paul's letter to the church at Galatia:

But now that faith has come, we are no longer subject to a disciplinarian, for in Christ Jesus you are all children of God through faith. As many of you as were baptized into Christ have clothed yourselves with Christ. There is no longer Jew or Greek, there is no longer slave or free, there is no longer male and female; for all of you are one in Christ Jesus.

Galatians 3.25–28

Symbolic prayer

Leader   That was Paul's letter. Now it's our turn to write a letter – a letter addressed to the opposite gender from ourselves. We will write them in the presence of God so that they become a form of prayer, a prayer that we are invited to share with the rest of the group.

The letters will, no doubt, take many different forms and will each come from your own perspective. They provide an opportunity to explore and express your thoughts and feelings raised by what you have heard. Perhaps you feel repentant, or angry, hopeful or empowered, sad or maybe confused. Whatever your feelings, consider what you would most like to say to members of your opposite gender. Try to write from the heart, but with compassion, too.

Take a pen and a card, with either a stereotypically blue ribbon if you are male and pink if you are female. When you have written your letter, which can remain anonymous, you are invited to tie it to the appropriate mannequin. After the service, take the opportunity to read and then reflect on the letters that have been written, particularly ones addressed to your own gender. Perhaps use what you read as a basis for further prayer and reflection.

Reflective music is either played or sung while the cards are being written and then tied to the mannequins.

Bible reading

Reader 1   These words come from 1 Corinthians:

Nevertheless, in the Lord woman is not independent of man or man independent of woman. For just as woman came from man, so man comes through woman; but all things come from God.

1 Corinthians 11.11–12

Prayer

Leader   And so we pray to the God of all reconciliation:

All   **Almighty and eternal God,**
high above all gender:
turn the hearts of men toward women,
and turn the hearts of women toward men.
Turn the hearts of rich toward poor,
and turn the hearts of poor toward rich.
Turn the heart of earth toward heaven,
for the heart of heaven is turned constantly toward earth,
until in you all people are one,
and the whole earth sings your praise.

Song of trust in God

Blessing

Men	A blessing on the men and on the women.
Women	A blessing on our bodies and on our souls.
Men	A blessing on our work and on our leisure.
Women	A blessing on the boys and on the girls.
Men	A blessing on our life and on our death.
Women	A blessing on all who cry out to Jesus.
All	A blessing this day and always. Amen.

Season of Remembrance

With the onset of autumn begins a season of remembrance. We look back on the summer as the leaves begin to fade and we enter into a season of reflection. Many churches celebrate the feast of All Saints and All Souls when we give thanks for the example of those who have gone before us, and pray for loved ones departed. We then move on to remembering more violent, divisive times – 'Remember, remember the 5th of November, gunpowder, treason and plot' – the attempt by the Roman Catholic Guy Fawkes to blow up the Protestant Houses of Parliament, shortly followed by Remembrance Day when we commemorate those who died in the wars of this and the last century, and pray for peace.

The three liturgies in this section focus on remembering those who live in situations of conflict and the resolve to work for peace and justice through reconciliation. The first reflects a specific situation, the occupied Palestinian territory. Although the second is born out of the trauma of South Africa's apartheid history, it can be adapted for use in other situations where reconciliation is desired; and the third liturgy is an Agape meal when we remember Christ's body broken for us and seek to literally 're-member', to come together as God's people and love as he loved us.

OFFERING AN OLIVE BRANCH

Preparation

You will need a small bowl with some olive oil in it, preferably Palestinian.

The Approach

Introduction

Leader   In this service we will pray for peace in the land that we call Holy. We will remember, in particular, Palestinian olive farmers living in occupied territory in the West Bank and Gaza, and we will pray with them for the restoration of justice and for reconciliation with their Israeli neighbours, so Palestinian and Israeli may live in peace.

Opening responses

Leader   Bless the Lord, O my Soul.
All   **O Lord, you are very great.**

Leader   You are clothed with honour and majesty,
All   **wrapped in light like a garment.**

Leader   You cause the grass to grow for the cattle
All   **and plants for people to use;**

Leader   Oil to make the face shine
All   **and bread to strengthen the human heart.**

Leader   The trees of the Lord are watered abundantly,
All   **the cedars of Lebanon that God planted.**

Leader   O Lord, how manifold are your works!
All   **In wisdom, you have made them all.**

Based on Psalm 104

Opening song

Reflection On olive trees in the occupied Palestinian territory

Reader   In the dark shadows
of trees like these
you cried for consolation.
On twisted trunks carved with age
you traced your pain.

Roots like these roots
received your tears.
May the abundant comfort
of ancient trees,
whose arms for you encompassed
all the world's agony,
become today's new harvest
of serenity and peace.

The Word

Reading

Reader   The Lord your God is bringing you into a good land, a land with flowing streams, with springs and underground waters welling up in valleys and hills, a land of wheat and barley, of vines and fig trees and pomegranates, a land of olive trees and honey, a land where you may eat bread without scarcity, where you will lack nothing. You shall eat your fill and bless the Lord your God for the good land that he has given you.

Deuteronomy 8.7–10

Story from the West Bank

Reader 1   Abu Saleem is 83 years old. He is a Palestinian Christian living in Beit Sahour next to Bethlehem. He has spent his life looking after olive trees – planting, growing, nurturing and harvesting them.

Reader 2   Since the beginning of the second intifada in September 2000 the Israeli military has uprooted or destroyed more than 400,000 olive trees.

Reader 1   To clear the land for the construction of the separation barrier in the West Bank, the Israeli army bulldozers came onto Abu Saleem's land between Jerusalem and Bethlehem and began to uproot the Olive trees that he grew.

Reader 2   Since the beginning of the second intifada in September 2000 the Israeli Defence Force has uprooted more than 450,000 citrus trees.

Reader 1   One of Abu Saleem's trees was over 1,000 years old. He called it 'mabroukeh', which means 'blessed'. It had been his grandfather's wish that the tree be cared for after he was gone and Abu Saleem was prepared to give his life to save it.

Reader 2   Since the beginning of the second intifada in September 2000 the Israeli Defence Force has uprooted more than 80,000 almond trees.

Reader 1   Abu Saleem turned down a payment of £300 for the olive tree. Many trees that are uprooted from Palestinian farms are simply taken from their owners and sold on to be planted in Israel.

Reader 2   Since the beginning of the second intifada in September 2000 the Israeli Defence Force has uprooted more than 20,000 banana trees and 30,000 palm trees.

Reader 1   Zechariah says: 'Wail, O cypress, for the cedar has fallen, for the glorious trees are ruined.'

Reader 2   'Wail, oaks of Bashan, for the thick forest has been felled.'

Song

Reading

Reader   The Lord your God is bringing you into a good land, a land with flowing streams, with springs and underground waters welling up in valleys and hills, a land of wheat and barley, of vines and fig trees and pomegranates, a land of olive trees and honey, a land where you may eat bread without scarcity, where you will lack nothing. You shall eat your fill and bless the Lord your God for the good land that he has given you.

Take care that you do not forget the Lord your God, by failing to keep his commandments, his ordinances, and his statutes, which I am commanding you today.

If you do forget the Lord your God and follow other gods to serve and worship them, I solemnly warn you today that you shall surely perish.

Deuteronomy 8.7–11 and 19

The Response

Confession

Leader   We confess that:
Rather than sing your worship
we have silenced creation's praise.
Rather than listen to the cries of the oppressed,
we have stopped our ears so they cannot hear.
Rather than see the poverty of the marginalized,
we have turned our eyes to easier views.
Rather than shout for justice and peace,
we have whispered, in case our opinions are unpopular.
Rather than act to bring about change,
we have busied ourselves with irrelevancies.
Rather than do your will,
we have done our own.

All   **Lord when we fail,
forgive us and renew us.
Inspire and challenge us
to be the people you want us to be.
Send us out into the world,
to strive again to be your children,
this day and all days.
Amen.**

Story of hope

Reader 1   Abu Nidal lives on the outskirts of Beit Jala, also very close to Bethlehem. Because of the separation barrier he has been prevented from travelling to his job in Jerusalem. So like many Palestinians he has turned to farming to feed his family.

Reader 2   The East Jerusalem YMCA and YWCA[1], both Christian Aid partners, run the Keep Hope Alive campaign which aims to replant 50,000 olive trees in the occupied Palestinian territory, so replacing the ones that have been uprooted by the Israeli army during military incursions or to build settlements or the separation barrier.

---

1 Young Men's Christian Association and Young Women's Christian Association respectively.

Reader 1   Abu Nidal moved to the area in 1977. He has all the right paperwork to prove that he owns the land that he farms, but because of the building of the separation barrier through it he will lose any chance to earn a living from it.

Reader 2   Planting olive trees helps farmers to earn a living from their land. It helps replace trees that have been uprooted by Israeli settlers or the Israelis military. But it is also about much more than that. It is about protesting against the destruction of farmland, while keeping farmland in use can in itself protect the land from confiscation by the Israeli authorities.

Reader 1   In 2008 the YMCA and YWCA planted 200 olive trees on Abu Nidal's land. Abu Nidal says 'If there are no houses or trees the land is much easier to grab. But it is much harder if the trees are planted by foreign sponsors.'

Reader 2   He goes on to say 'When I get such support, I feel that hope is still alive. It is not the money or the trees themselves, but the fact that there still exist people who care, who care whether Palestinians are able to stay on their own land.'

Intercessions

Between each bidding use a sung response, such as 'O Lord, hear our prayer' or 'Through our lives and by our prayers, your kingdom come.'

Leader   Let us pray:
For Palestinians whose lives and livelihoods have been destroyed along with their homes and farms, uprooted by bulldozers and crushed by occupation.
Lord, do not let their hopes be crushed or their futures be uprooted but stand with them now.

Sung response

For Israelis and Palestinians, both victims of this conflict, whose friends and family have been killed in the violence.
Lord, do not let their love die with those they have loved and lost, but grant them the strength to love when hate seems so much easier.

Sung response

> For all who work for peace in the land we call holy, who have seen their dreams broken again and again.
>
> Lord, grant them strength to hold on to their vision of a restored land and a reconciled people.

Sung response

> For ourselves when we feel powerless to help.
>
> Lord, help us to know that our prayers and our actions stand in unity with all who hurt and yet struggle for peace, now and always.

Sung response

Signing with oil

Reader   How very good and pleasant it is
when kindred live together in unity!
It is like the precious oil on the head,
running down upon the beard,
on the beard of Aaron,
running down over the collar of his robes.
It is like the dew of Hermon,
which falls on the mountains of Zion.
For there the Lord ordained his blessing,
life for evermore.

Psalm 133

Leader   As a sign of our desire for unity with one another, and of our solidarity with Israelis and Palestinians struggling for peace and justice, you are invited to anoint your neighbour by dipping your finger in a small bowl of Palestinian Olive oil, which will be passed round, and signing their forehead with the sign of the cross, using the words 'May God bless you.'

As the oil is passed round, reflective music can be played or a repetitive song or chant sung.

Prayer for unity

All Pray not for Arab or Jew
    for Palestinian or Israeli
    but pray rather for ourselves
    that we might not divide them in our prayers
    but keep them both together in out hearts.
    Amen.

Blessing

Closing song

RITE OF RECONCILIATION AND HEALING

This rite of reconciliation was put together by the South African Council of Churches in response to the work of the Truth and Reconciliation Commission, which sought to reconcile and heal a traumatized nation. Believing that the truth sets us free, it saw the work of the Commission as a practical expression of a religious understanding about the way we deal with one another as God's people.

  The Rite of Reconciliation provides a way of coming before God in repentance, receiving forgiveness and experiencing reconciliation with God and one another.

Preparation

Because this service uses fire, it is recommended that the worship happens outdoors.

You will need:
✠ means of making a small fire
✠ oil for anointing.

Call to worship

Leader The world belongs to God
All   the earth and all its people.

Leader How good and how lovely it is
All   to live together in unity.

Leader	Love and faith come together,
All	justice and peace join hands.

Leader	If the Lord's disciples kept silent
All	these stones would shout aloud.

Leader	Lord, open our lips
All	and our mouths shall proclaim your praise.

Based on Psalm 133

Song of praise or adoration

Reading

Address or reflection

Penitential rite

The leader may use these or other related passages from scripture:

Leader   Jesus said, 'Come to me all who labour and are heavy laden, and I will give you rest.'

Matthew 11.28

Jesus said, 'Do not let your hearts be troubled, trust in God, trust also in me.'

John 14.1

'If we say we have no sin, we deceive ourselves, and the truth is not in us. If we confess our sins, he is faithful and just, and will forgive our sins and cleanse us from all unrighteousness.'

1 John 1.8, 9

Act of penitence

Leader   God Almighty, we acknowledge that we stood by help-lessly when the dwellings of the innocent were cast down (Jeremiah 9.19). When land was joined to land, we ignored the cries of the innocent.

Silence

Leader   Lord, have mercy.
All   **Christ, have mercy.**

Leader   We stood by when innocent children were killed in cold blood.

Silence

Leader   Lord, have mercy.
All   **Christ, have mercy.**

Leader   You asked about my sister and brother and I rudely answered, 'I do not know; Am I my sister's and brother's keeper?'

Genesis 4.9

Silence

Leader   Lord, have mercy.
All   **Christ, have mercy.**

Leader   You have commanded, 'You shall not kill' (Exodus 20.13), yet we took up arms to defend apartheid and mercilessly killed innocent people.

Silence

Leader   Lord, have mercy.
All   **Christ, have mercy.**

Leader   We wrongly informed on our sisters and brothers who were part of the struggle for our freedom.

Silence

Leader   Lord, have mercy.
All   **Christ, have mercy.**

Leader   We enjoyed the privileges of education, employment and land while others went without.

Silence

Leader   Lord, have mercy.
All   **Christ, have mercy.**

Leader   We hurt each other deeply. Now we ask for healing.

Silence

Leader   Lord, have mercy.
All   **Christ, have mercy.**

The Act of Penitence is followed by a period of silence. Anyone who wishes to is then invited to make an open confession.

Communal Confession

All   **Merciful God, in your goodness, forgive us our sins, against the unity of your family. Make us one in heart, one in spirit. Remove the blindness of our hearts and minds. Forgive us our wrong doings and reconcile us to yourself. We ask this through Christ our Lord. Amen.**

Cleansing rite

With the use of the symbols below or other symbols, those present can respond by participating in the ceremony of cleansing and healing.

Cleansing rite using fire

Blessing of the fire

Leader   Father, we share the light of your glory through your Son the light of the world. Sanctify this fire and inflame us with new hope through Jesus Christ our Lord. Amen.

The leader says the following prayer and a representative group of participants comes forward and places their outstretched hands momentarily over the fire.

Leader   Holy Father,
       with this fire, cleanse the stains of our souls.
All   **Christ, hear us.**

Leader   With this fire, burn down the walls of division among us.
All   **Lord, hear us.**

Leader   With this fire, purify us so that your Word may find a clean
       abode in us.
All   **Christ, hear us.**

Leader   With this fire, test our feeble faith and do not find us
       wanting.
All   **Lord, hear us.**

Leader   With this fire, inspire us with courage to embrace the truth.
       Drive out the fear from our hearts.
All   **Christ, hear us.**

Leader   With this fire, let us feel each other's warmth. Drive out the
       ghost of the past.
All   **Lord, hear us.**

Leader   With this fire, light our path. Rekindle our fervour. Set our
       hearts aflame.
All   **Christ, hear us.**

Leader   Renew a zeal in us to build a new flame.
All   **Lord, hear us.**

Leader   We ask this, through Christ our Lord.
All   **Amen.**

Absolution

Leader   Almighty God, who forgives all who truly repent, have
       mercy upon us; pardon our sins and set us free from them;
       confirm and strengthen us in all goodness and keep us in
       eternal life; through Jesus Christ our Lord.
All   **Amen.**

Song of praise and thanksgiving

Oil of healing

Leader   Are any among you suffering? They should pray. Are any cheerful? They should sing songs of praise. Are any among you sick? They should call for the elder of the church and have them pray over them, anointing them with oil in the name of the Lord. The prayer of faith will save the sick, and the Lord will raise them up; and anyone who has committed sins will be forgiven.

    Therefore, confess your sins to one another, and pray for one another, so that you may be healed. The prayer of the righteous is powerful and effective.

James 5.13–16

Those who wish to are invited to come to the front of the worship area and sign each other on the forehead with oil.

Sharing of the peace

Leader   How very good and pleasant it is
        when kindred live together in unity!
    It is like the precious oil on the head,
        running down upon the beard,
    on the beard of Aaron,
        running down over the collar of his robes.
    It is like the dew of Hermon,
        which falls on the mountains of Zion.
    For there the Lord ordained his blessing,
        life for evermore.

Psalm 133

Everyone is invited to share the Peace.

Concluding prayer

Blessing

Dismissal

Leader   Jesus declared, 'Go now and leave your life of sin.'

(John 8.11)

RITES OF CLEANSING

Libation Rite

In South Africa, a libation is made out of beer, blood or water and mixed with mealie meal in a calabash (a bowl made from a hollowed out gourd). The libation represents the ancestors and spirits of those who have died unjustly as victims or defenders of the apartheid government.

To fit our own different context, an alternative mixture could be made – perhaps out of wine, water and bread, for example, to represent injured parties or the lives of those lost in an act of violence or as a result of some conflict.

As the minister says the following prayer, adapted to fit our cultural context, the libation is poured over a weapon, or whatever has afflicted a wound, which is lain ceremoniously on a blanket or cloth in the centre of the floor.

Prayer

Leader   As we pour out this libation, we call to mind those who have died in acts of violence or have been hurt at our hands or by our collusion, and we remember them now.

We remember those who have died before their time as innocent victims of human blindness; all those who died because they unknowingly defended a cruel political order; all those who have died because we failed to intervene; those who have been injured at our hands; those who have been hurt because we stood by and watched; those who have been injured because we turned away.

We call for God's strength to face one another as members of his family.

We ask Christ Jesus, the atonement of our sins, to plead for us with the Father.

We ask for truth and simplicity of heart.

We ask for compassion and mercy.

We ask for the capacity to forgive and to accept forgiveness.

We ask for courage and honesty through Christ our Lord.

Amen.

Cleansing rite using water

In this rite, the congregation is invited to wash their hands in a bowl of water. A helper then dries each person's hands with a towel. Alternatively, the minister or priest, at his or her discretion, may sprinkle the congregation with water.

Blessing of the water prayer

Leader   Holy Father
With this water, cool our hands, our bodies from the heat of the sun.
All   **Christ, have mercy.**

Leader   With this water, kindly remove the heat of the heart.
All   **Lord, have mercy.**

Leader   With this water, soothe our injured feelings; remove the anger of yesterday.
All   **Christ, have mercy.**

Leader   Cleanse us from true and false accusation.
All   **Lord, have mercy.**

Leader   Cleanse the stains left by our own wrongdoing.
All   **Christ, have mercy.**

Leader   Wash away the bloodstains of those who have died unjustly.
All   **Lord, have mercy.**

Leader   Purify our hearts and minds.
All   **Christ, have mercy.**

Leader   Remove any traces of suspicion.
All   **Lord, have mercy.**

Leader   With this water, give a fresh start to build a new community.
All   **Christ, have mercy.**

Leader   With this water, fill our hearts with a clean spirit.
All   **Lord, have mercy.**

Leader   With this water, prepare us to be reconciled to yourself through Christ and through one another and to one another.

All   Amen.

Cleansing rite using stones

In South Africa, a goat may be used in a rite of cleansing, in a similar way a scapegoat was used in the Old Testament to bear the sins of the people. As an alternative to a goat, a stone could be laid down after each bidding to symbol the laying down of a burden.

All   **Lord, have mercy.**

Leader   For the division caused by . . . .
All   **Christ, have mercy.**

Leader   For the misunderstanding caused by . . . .
All   **Lord, have mercy.**

Leader   For the hurt caused by . . . .
All   **Christ, have mercy.**

Leader   For the anger caused by . . . .
All   **Lord, have mercy.**

Leader   For the discrimination caused by . . . .
All   **Christ, have mercy.**

Leader   For the persecution caused by . . . .
All   **Lord, have mercy.**

Leader   With our lips, we claimed to be members of the Body of Christ but denied it in our actions.
All   **Christ, have mercy.**

Leader   We now ask for forgiveness and reconciliation.
All   **Lord, have mercy.**

Leader   We ask for strength not to indulge in the wrongs of the past.
All   **Christ, have mercy.**

Leader   May we experience again the mercy of God.
All   **Christ, have mercy.**

Leader	We ask this through Jesus Christ, our Lord.
All	**Amen.**

Cleansing rite using oil

In South Africa, bile or gall is used in this cleansing rite. An alternative to this could be olive oil or equivalent.

As the foreheads of the congregation are signed with the cross in oil, the following prayer is said:

Leader	With this oil, anoint the wounds of division amongst us.
All	**Christ, have mercy.**
Leader	Soothe the pain that has exhausted and diminished us.
All	**Lord, have mercy.**
Leader	With this oil, let our hearts and minds be transformed by hope.
All	**Christ, have mercy.**
Leader	Protect us from the evil that tried to destroy your image in us.
All	**Lord, have mercy.**
Leader	With this oil, strengthen and guide us.
All	**Christ, have mercy.**
Leader	Heal our minds and bodies that we may be bearers of reconciliation.
All	**Lord, have mercy.**
Leader	With this oil, we lift our hearts to you in prayer, O Lord.
All	**Christ, have mercy.**
Leader	Anoint us to carry your healing touch wherever we go.
All	**Lord, have mercy.**
Leader	We ask this through Christ, our Lord.

LOVE ONE ANOTHER – AN AGAPE MEAL

Whenever Christians share in a service of Holy Communion, the Eucharist or Mass they remember the last supper Jesus had with his disciples and his body broken on the cross. Breaking bread together in an Agape meal, a meal shared in love, as its name suggests, is a way Christians can recognize their brokenness and divisions in the knowledge of the reconciling love of God which brings healing. An Agape offers a way to be re-membered literally, to come together to love as Christ first loved us.

Call to worship

All   As we gather together here today,
we commit ourselves to you once again, O God.
We commit ourselves to one another,
and we pray that we may be created anew
to share in Christ's redeeming work.

Opening hymn or song

Opening words

All   God of life,
God of many names,
Creator, Mother, Father,
God of Jesus Christ,
Rabbi of the poor,
receive our praise and worship.
Your breath gives us life and being,
your love breaks our dividing walls
and you walk with us to freedom.
God of wounded hands,
carpenter of new creation,
out of struggle, confusion, despair,
we cry out that your life
gives hope to our world.
Womb and birth of joy
we celebrate your reign,
for you bring down

the mighty from their thrones,
you lift up the lowly
and fill the hungry with good things.

Hymn or song

The Word

Reading

Reader   As the Father has loved me, so I have loved you; abide in
my love. If you keep my commandments, you will abide in
my love, just as I have kept my Father's commandments and
abide in his love. I have said these things to you so that my
joy may be in you, and that your joy may be complete.

'This is my commandment, that you love one another
as I have loved you. No one has greater love than this, to
lay down one's life for one's friends. You are my friends if
you do what I command you. I do not call you servants any
longer, because the servant does not know what the master
is doing; but I have called you friends, because I have made
known to you everything that I have heard from my Father.
You did not choose me but I chose you. And I appointed you
to go and bear fruit, fruit that will last, so that the Father
will give you whatever you ask him in my name. I am giving
you these commands so that you may love one another.

John 15.9–17

Silence

Short address or reflection

Confession

Leader   If we confess our sins,
God is just and may be trusted to forgive us
and cleanse us from every kind of wrong.

All   **For our incapacity to feel the sufferings of others,
and our tendency to live comfortably with injustice,
God forgive us.**

For the self-righteousness which denies guilt,
and the self-interest which strangles compassion,
God forgive us.
For the times we are
too eager to be better than others,
too rushed to care,
too tired to bother,
when we don't really listen,
when we are too quick to act from
motives other than love,
God forgive us.
For our failings in community,
our lack of understanding and forgiveness,
our insensitivity,
we ask your mercy.
For our domination of the earth
and our exploitation of your creation,
God forgive us.

Intercessions

All   We pray to you, O God,
Leader for the Church and all who believe,
        that your will be done.

All   We pray to you, O God,
Leader for those in leadership positions,
        that government may be justly administered.

All   We pray to you, O God,
Leader for all who live with the legacy of injustice
        and discrimination.

All   We pray to you, O God,
Leader for those caught up in conflict and violence
        in our world today.

All   We pray to you, O God,
Leader for all those working for peace
        in our country and elsewhere,
        and for ourselves that we may be peace-makers
        in thought, word and deed.

All	We pray to you, O God,
Leader	for prisoners everywhere, especially those condemned to death,
	and for their family and friends.

All	We pray to you, O God,
Leader	for those who live in poverty
	and those who are unemployed, homeless or refugees.

All	We pray to you, O God,
Leader	for those who are sick, infirm or lonely
	and for those who mourn or are in any distress.

All	We pray to you, O God,
Leader	for wholeness and healing in ourselves,
	in our communities and our country.

All	We pray to you, O God,
Leader	for the integrity of creation,
	and for its healing and restoration.

All	We pray to you, O God ...

Continue with free prayer if appropriate and bring to a close with the following prayer:

All	Eternal Spirit, life-giver, pain-bearer, lovemaker,
	source of all that is and that shall be,
	Father and Mother of us all,
	Loving God, in whom is heaven,
	the hallowing of your name echo through the universe,
	the way of your justice be followed by
	the peoples of the world.
	Your heavenly will be done by all created beings.
	Your kingdom of peace and freedom
	sustain our hope and come on earth.
	With the bread that we need for today, feed us.
	For the hurts that we inflict on one another, forgive us.
	In times of temptation and test, strengthen us.
	From trials too great to endure, spare us.
	From the grip of all that is evil, free us.

**For you reign in the glory of the power that is love
now and for ever. Amen.**

Jim Cotter

The Peace

Leader   'I give you a new commandment:
Love one another;
Just as I have loved you,
You must also love one another;
By this love you have for one another
Everyone will know that you are my disciples.'

John 13.34–5

Pass the Peace

Prayer of Blessing over the offertory bowl

Leader   Lord,
bless this bowl,
bless the hands that made it,
that shaped it and fashioned it.
Bless the hands that hold it,
that invite prayer and giving.
Bless the hands that will touch it as they give,
that pass it to their neighbours.
Lord, bless this bowl.
Amen.

*The bowl can then be used to receive the Offering and can also be used
to hold the bread for the shared meal.*

The Meal

Leader   O risen Christ, you made yourself known
to the disciples in the breaking of bread at Emmaus.
The bread that we break together this day
is a sign of the brokenness of the world.
Through our sharing in the bread of life
in our many Christian communities,
open our eyes and hands to the needs of all people.

Let our hearts burn to share your gifts
and help us to go forth with one another
and with bread: bread of hope, bread of life and bread of
peace.

The passing of the bread and wine

Each person passes the bread to their neighbour saying: 'Name ... the
food of fellowship' (or hope, or life or peace).
   Each person passes the wine to their neighbour, saying: 'Name ... the
drink of fellowship' (or hope, or life or peace).

Thanksgiving

All   We thank you that, in your Spirit,
people have lived courageously,
people have sought your freedom,
people have caught your vision.
We thank you that you make us in your image,
that you came to live among us
that we, too, may live in your light.
Amen.

Hymn or song

Commissioning

All   Loving God,
direct us in ways we do not yet discern,
equip us for the service of reconciliation
and true liberation in your world.
May there be peace wherever people live,
the peace that we cannot make ourselves,
the power of Christ Jesus here among us.

Leader   Let us go forth into the world
All   in your name. Amen.

General Services

AN ORDER FOR MORNING PRAYER

The Approach

Call to worship

Leader   Come Uvenlingqaki – the First One!
Come Ukulunkulu – the Great One!

Come Modimo – the High One!
Come Modiri – the Maker of All Things!

Come Lesa – the Spirit that Gives Life!

God's presence is acknowledged:

Sunday

Leader   In the beginning was the Word,
All   **and the Word was with God, and the Word was God.**

(John 1.1)

Monday

Leader   And a voice came from heaven:
All   **'You are my Child; with you I am well pleased.'**

(Mark 1.11)

Tuesday

Leader   The voice of one crying out in the wilderness:
All   **'Prepare the way of the Lord, make God's path straight!'**

(Matthew 3.3)

Wednesday

Leader   'Blessed are you who are poor;
All   **for yours is the kingdom of God.'**

(Luke 6.20)

Thursday

Leader   'Ask and it will be given you;
All   **search, and you will find;**
Leader   knock and the door will be opened for you.
All   **For everyone who asks, receives, and everyone who**
          searches, finds.'

(Matthew 7.7–8)

Friday

Leader   'I saw the Lord always before me;
All   **so God is near me and so I will not be troubled.'**

(Acts 2.25)

Saturday

Leader   You show me the path of life;
All   **in your presence is the fullness of joy.**

(Psalm 16.11)

The time of devotion is offered to Jesus by the lighting of a candle.

Leader   Jesus Christ, Light of the World, you shine upon us.
          Jesus Christ, Light of the World, the darkness has never
          overcome you.
          Jesus Christ, Light of the World, grant us peace.

God is praised in song or the Psalm appointed for the day is read.

The prayer of the morning

Leader   At the dawning of this day,
Lord of Life, touch us.
Open our souls to your transforming Spirit,
so that today, through us,
your kingdom will come, and your will be done.
So be it! Amen.

The Ministry of the Word

Reading and reflection

A passage of scripture is read followed by a time of reflection.

The following four questions may be used to aid reflection:

- *What does this passage tell me about God?*
- *What does it tell me about humanity?*
- *What does it tell me about the relationship between God and humanity?*
- *In the light of these three questions, what does God want me to do today?*

Response to the Word

God is praised through the Te Deum Laudamus, or another prayer or song.

Leader   We praise you, O God, we proclaim you Lord;
All   **all creation worships you, the one who gives us life.**

Leader   All the angels worship you, and the saints in glory join in,
together praising your holy name.
All   **'Holy, holy, holy Lord,**
God of power and might,
heaven and earth overflow with your glory!'

Leader   Those who serve your Church as apostles praise you.
Those who fulfil your ministry as prophets praise you.
Those who have died in your service and love praise you.
Your holy Church throughout the world acclaims you:
All   **Creator, God of eternal glory!**

Christ, the Saviour, worthy of all praise!
The Holy Spirit, advocate and guide!

Leader   You, Christ, are the King of Glory,
            the eternal Son of the living God.
            When you became like us to set us free,
            you humbly chose a virgin's womb.

All   **You overcame the eternal finality of death**
            and opened the Kingdom of Heaven to all who believe.

Leader   You are seated at God's right hand in glory.
            We believe you will come to be our judge.

All   **Come soon, O Lord, and save those who love you,**
            who have been bought with your precious blood,
            and bring us with all your saints to your eternal glory.

Leader   Save your people, O Lord, and bless all whom you love.
All   **Guide and intercede for us eternally.**

Leader   Day by day we bless you.
All   **We praise your name for ever.**

Leader   Today, Lord Jesus, keep us from all sin,
All   **Have mercy on us, Lord, have mercy.**

Leader   Show us your love and mercy,
All   **for we put our trust in you.**

Leader   In you, Lord, is our hope,
            never let us be ashamed of you!

God's world is prayed for

Prayers of intercession are offered, using this form, or extempore.

Leader   We bring our needs and the needs of the world, so that all
            may be ordered to your perfect will.
            We pray for the world . . .
            We pray for the Church . . .
            We pray for those whom we love . . .
            We pray for those we struggle to love . . .
            We bring these needs before you . . .

Silence

Leader   God of mercy and grace,
you have heard these dreams, desires and needs.
Help us to live as your answer to these prayers today,
and those things which we cannot do, transform them
by the miracle of your presence.
We ask this in Jesus' name.
So be it. Amen!

All   Our Father . . .

Dismissal

Final blessing

Leader   Living Lord,
live in us today.
Let your grace flow through us;
let your wisdom guide us;
let your presence be seen in us;
to the glory of your name.
So be it! Amen.

AN ORDER FOR EVENING PRAYER

The Approach

Call to worship

Leader   Come, bless the Lord, all you servants of the Lord,
All   **who stand by night in the house of the Lord!**
Leader   Lift up your hands to the holy place
All   **and bless the Lord.**
Leader   May the Lord, maker of heaven and earth,
All   **bless you in love.**

God's presence is acknowledged:

Sunday

Leader   From the rising of the sun to its setting,
All   **the name of the Lord is to be praised.**

(Psalm 113.3)

Monday

Leader   'I came that they may have life,
All   **And have it abundantly.'**

(John 10.10)

Tuesday

Leader   'Do not fear, for I have redeemed you;
All   **I have called you by name, you are mine.'**

(Isaiah 43.1)

Wednesday

Leader   'And remember, I am with you always,
All   **to the end of the age.'**

(Matthew 28.20)

Thursday

Leader   If God is for us, who is against us?
All   **Who shall separate us from the love of Christ?**

(Romans 8.31, 35)

Friday

Leader   The Lord will keep you from all evil;
All   **he will keep your life.**
Leader   The Lord will keep your going out and your coming in
All   **from this time forth forevermore.**

(Psalm 121.8)

Saturday

Leader   Blessed are the pure in heart,
All   **for they will see God.**

(Matthew 5.8)

God's forgiveness is received

Time is spent in silent reflection on the day that is drawing to a close.

Leader   Lord God, Creator, Saviour, and Lord,
we confess to you that we have sinned,
in thought, and word, and deed;
in the things we have said and done,
and the things we have not said or done.
Please forgive us for our sins,
recreate us in the power of your spirit,
and raise us to new life in Jesus Christ the Lord.

Scripture says:
'If we confess our sins,
the God who is faithful and just will forgive us our sins
and cleanse us from all unrighteousness.' (I John 1.19)

So be it! Thanks be to God. Amen.

God is praised

God is praised in song or the psalm appointed for the day is read.

The Prayer of the Evening

Leader   O God, who created both night and day,
the one who never slumbers nor sleeps;
Flood us with your holy presence,
that in this night, as throughout this day,
we may be filled with your peace,
in Jesus Christ our Lord.
So be it! Amen.

Ministry of the Word

Reading and reflection

The passage from scripture read in the morning is read again, followed by time to reflect on how it has impacted on the day.

If Morning Prayer was not kept, the passage is read and the four questions reflected upon:

- *What does this passage tell me about God?*
- *What does it tell me about humanity?*
- *What does it tell me about the relationship between God and humanity?*
- *In the light of these three questions, what does God want me to do today?*

Response to the Word

God is praised through the Magnificat (the Song of Mary in Luke 1.46–55) or the Nunc Dimittis (the Song of Simeon in Luke 2.29–32).

The Magnificat

Leader	My soul magnifies the Lord, and my spirit rejoices in God my Saviour, for God has looked with favour on the lowliness of his servant.
All	**Surely, from now on all generations will call me blessed; for the mighty has done great things for me, and holy is his name.**
Leader	His mercy is for those who fear him from generation to generation.
All	**He has shown strength with his arm; he has scattered the proud in the thoughts of their hearts. He has brought down the powerful from their thrones, and lifted up the lowly;**
Leader	he has filled the hungry with good things, and sent the rich away empty.
All	**He has helped his servant Israel, in remembrance of his mercy, according to the promise he made to our ancestors, to Abraham and to his descendants for ever.**

The Nunc Dimittis

Leader	Master, now you are dismissing your servant in peace, according to your word;
All	**for my eyes have seen your salvation which you have prepared in the presence of all peoples:**
Leader	A light for revelation to the Gentiles, and for glory to your people Israel.

The day is closed in prayer

Prayers of thanksgiving and intercession are offered, using this form, or extempore:

Leader   Lord God, Creator of the day that is now closing,
             we thank you for this day –
All   **for all who shared it, enabling us to see you afresh;**
Leader   for your presence in all that happened;
             and for your Spirit guiding us in your will.

Leader   We bring to you all who will struggle with sleep tonight –
All   **those who do not sleep comfortably;**
             the many whose hunger will make sleep difficult;
             those who are fearful to close their eyes;
             and the sick, the ill and the depressed.

Leader   We bring before you, too, those who stay awake so that we
             may sleep –
All   **the police and those ensuring our security;**
             those who tend the sick and care for the hurting;
             engineers and workers who keep our country running;
             and those who prepare for my life tomorrow.

Leader   We commit into your gracious keeping all whom we love
             . . .
             those who lead us as a country, a community and a Church
             . . .
             the children and youth who look forward to tomorrow . . .
             the aged, many of whom dread another new day . . .
             and those who will pass into a New Day this night . . .

             We bring all our worries, cares and prayers to you,
             in Jesus' name,
             So be it! Amen.

All   **Our Father . . .**

Final blessing

Leader   Living Lord,
            as you have guided, led and blessed us today –
            may your love calm our fears;
            your Spirit keep us safe
            and your grace give us rest this night;
            to the glory of your name.
            So be it! Amen.

A CHILDREN'S SERVICE

The Approach

*The start of the service is announced with the beating of a drum or
another clear symbol.*

We are welcomed

Leader   When Jesus was on earth, he often spent time with
               children:
            'Bring children to me,' he said:
All   **'For God's eternal home is theirs forever!'**

Leader   We gather to worship God as the one who creates all
               things,
            who forgives us when we do wrong things,
All   **and who fills our lives with real love!**

We praise God in song

An appropriate song is sung.

We praise God in prayer

Leader   Lord God, you have made all things:
            from the highest mountain to the deepest sea,
            the giraffe so tall and the lizard so small,
All   **I love you, my God – for you also made me!**

Leader	Lord Jesus, you came to show me your love:
	you lived your life so full and so free,
	you fed the hungry and healed the sick,
All	**I love you, Lord Jesus – for you also love me!**

Leader	Holy Spirit, you come and live in my heart:
	your love in my life I can always see
	as you grow in my heart to be like you,
All	**I love you, my God – for you also grow me!**

We praise God in song

An appropriate song is sung.

We tell God we are sorry for all we do wrong

The congregation are led in prayers of confession and absolution, either with these words, or extempore.

Leader	Lord God, we thank you for loving us each day,
	for giving us this beautiful world,
	for food, clothes and friends to play with.
	for our parents and family and everything else,
All	**'thank you' are the only words we can say!**

Leader	But we know that we often forget to love you:
	we waste all you give us and litter your earth,
	we fight and we scream, and hurt others too,
	we think of ourselves and forget about them,
All	**'we are sorry, Lord, what can we do?'**

Leader	Now we hear God speak to our hearts:
	'I love you, my child, you are my own,
	I don't want us ever to be far apart,
	I forgive you all you've done wrong!'
All	**Come, Lord Jesus, and fill up my heart!**

We bring God our offerings and gifts

As well as money, or instead of money, children can bring up things they have made such as drawings and collages, nature treasures they have found, and so on.

An appropriate song is sung while the Offering is taken.

The Offering is received, and thanks given:

Leader   Lord God, we thank you for your love today:
for this world and for everything in it.
We bring you our gifts and the things we've made,
and pray that we may learn to share with others
all the good things you have given us.

The ministry of the Word

If age-appropriate, a short scripture lesson is read.

We thank God for the Word in song

An appropriate song is sung.

We hear God's Good News

A message is shared or a story told.

The response

An appropriate song is sung.

We now pray for God's World.

Leader
All   Lord God, we bring your world to you in prayer:
we pray for those places with too much rain,
and places that need to feel rain again.
also for countries where hate makes them kill,
and then all the places where your earth is ill.

Leader
All   We pray for people who don't feel your love:
fill everyone who is sad with your love,
touch all the sick with your hand from above,
those who are hungry, please let them have food,
to all who are lonely, a friend who is good.

Leader
All   Lord Jesus, we come to pray for our land,
our homes and our schools and our hospitals, too,
may they all reflect the presence of you!
We pray for the children throughout our bright land,
'Please keep them safe in your strong, loving hand.'

Leader   We ask all our prayers in Jesus' name,
          As we join in saying the prayer that he gave us as his
          family:

All   Our Father ...

Dismissal

A happy song is sung

The final blessing

All   And now may the awesome happiness of our Lord Jesus
              Christ,
          the amazing love of God,
          and the special friendship of the Holy Spirit,
          be with us all.
          So be it! Amen.

*The service is drawn to a close with the beating of the drum, or with the
congregation leaving in happy song.*

Part Two

Prayers

OPENING PRAYERS

We come together to declare the goodness of God,
to proclaim the body of Christ,
to celebrate the presence of the Spirit.

We come together to recognize the Godhead,
to declare God's glory in the heavens,
to welcome God to this place on earth.

We come as we are to the God who is;
We await and will not be disappointed.

This is our space;
Let us use it to worship GOD on earth.

Christian Aid

Come Lord, share this time with us
just as you share our lives every day,
with light and shadow,
with music and joyful songs filling the air
and with, at other times, the sad wail of the soul
suffering without hope.
Come, Lord, share this time with us
just as one day you shared the dusty paths of life
with men, children and women,
preaching, healing, suffering, dying, loving,
raised up to keep alive hope in your new reign
we keep seeking.

Come, Lord, share this time with us
just as you shared words, gestures, hugs
and a real loaf of bread broken in pieces,
a sign of your complete commitment
to a world hungry for peace, justice and life.
Come, Lord, share this time with us.

**Mark us with the fire of your presence
transforming and renewing our lives.**

World AIDS Day, Ecumenical Advocacy Alliance

Holy God, you created one humanity.
Although our languages may differ and our skin colour vary,
all blood is red and all people bear your image.
Hallowed be your name.
Hallowed be your name.

Through Jesus, you created one Church.
Although our liturgies may differ and our theologies vary,
we are one in the body of Christ. We are all joined together.
Hallowed be your name.
Hallowed be your name.

Your spirit moves earth towards one future.
Although our desires differ and our politics vary,
we shall share one eternity, if only we let heaven happen here.
Hallowed be your name.
Hallowed be your name.

Christian Aid

Creator God,
We come to this place,
remembering your presence.
We come with our failings,
knowing we are welcome.
We come with our gifts,
offering them for your purpose.
We come with our dreams,
hoping you will make them new.

Here, in this place of meeting,
we take time together with friend and stranger
for when paths cross and pilgrims gather,
there is much to share and celebrate.

Christian Aid

God calls us together.
We're here.
God calls us to be still.
We'll pause.
God calls us to hear his word.
We'll listen.
God calls us to understand.
We'll try.
God calls us to act.
We're willing.

Christian Aid

The earth belongs to God, the world and all its people.
All power belongs to God,
who reigns above all nations.

The harvests of the earth sustain all men and women.
The wealth of every nation
must prosper every child.

The politics of earth are scrutinized in heaven.
God holds the scales of justice
and notes each threat to peace.

In Jesus, God revealed that all of life is sacred.
God's spirit knows no bounds
in making all things new.

Christian Aid

Let all that is visible worship the Lord:
High mountain ranges and leaves on the tree,
Microscopic creatures, sky-scraping towers,
Smile on the face and kiss on the lips,
Colours of the rainbow, people of the nations,
Lightning and landscape, sunset and shadow.
Let all that is visible worship the Lord.
Greatly give praise to the One who created you.

Let all that's invisible worship the Lord:
Life-giving oxygen, cool of the breeze,

Electrical current and radio waves,
Scent of the flower and taste on the tongue,
Burning emotion, mysterious sleep,
Silence and gravity, music and laughter.
Let all that's invisible worship the Lord.
Greatly give praise to the One who created you.

Christian Aid

Our help is in the name of the eternal God
who is making the heavens and the earth.

God of love, thank you for all that is good,
for our creation and our humanity,
for our roles as stewards of your earth,
for your gift of life and for one another,
for your love which is unbounded and eternal
and for your continued presence with us now.
O Lord, most holy and beloved,
our companion and our guide along the way;
we praise and thank you.
God of love, we adore you.
You strive with our resistant clay
and transform our hardened hearts
to bring harmony out of chaos.
God of love, we adore you.

South African Council of Churches

Men	For all who reach out to God that they may find him.
Women	For those who think they possess God that they may seek him.
Men	For all who fear the future that they may have confidence.
Women	For all who doubt that they may not despair.
Men	For all who wander aimlessly that they may find a fixed abode.
Women	For the lonely that they may meet another.

Men	For all who constantly hunger that they may be satisfied.
Women	For those who have enough to eat that they may discover what it is to be hungry.
Men	For those for whom all goes well that they may not become hard hearted.
Women	For the powerful that they may be aware that they are vulnerable.
Men	For all who live in this world between hope and fear.
All	**Free us from fear and from a false sense of security and give us all those things that are for our good through Jesus Christ our Lord. Amen.**

South African Council of Churches

CONFESSION AND ABSOLUTION

Loving God,
you make us in your image:
forgive us
when we fail to see you in each other,
when we give into greed and indifference,
when we fail to question the systems that are life-denying.
Help us
to live in your image,
to be Christ-like in service,
to love as he first loved us.
Amen.

Christian Aid (adapted)

All-knowing God:
we have treated people as less than human;
we have treated people as more than human.
we have belittled, exalted and envied others.
we have failed to stand up for ourselves and others in the face of evil.
we have denied our humanity and refused redemption.

Forgiving God,
we seek your love.

Empowering God,
we are truly sorry and turn to you.

God of grace and truth,
by your grace I am what I am.
I receive your grace.
God is faithful and just and forgives us.

South African Council of Churches

Merciful God, we confess that too often
we have closed our ears to the sound of children crying;
we have closed our eyes to the splendour of the angels;
we have closed our mouths and not spoken out for justice and peace.
Forgive us Lord,
and help us to share the joy of your presence. Amen.

Christian Aid

Eternal God,
We confess to you our sinfulness.
You made the world a paradise
but we have turned our lands into
places of tears and unhappiness.

People are fighting with each other,
race against race.
The holocaust of chauvinism
sweeps through countries
devouring humanity,
terrorising us into submission.

Liberating One,
free us from all bondage
so that our faith in you
will make us free
to create with courage
a new world –
new societies.

Sri Lanka

Lord God,
We repent of our denial and complacency in the face of HIV and AIDS
and our failure to respond to the challenge we face.
We acknowledge our prejudices and our fear as
we re-commit ourselves to communicating God's grace to the world
by identifying with those in need and ministering to them.

Open our hearts to your love and forgiveness
and empower us to bring change to your world.
Give us the grace to lead by example
That our families, communities and our nation
May be moved to serve one another in your name. Amen.

Diakonia Council of Churches, South Africa

Merciful God,
you keep your promise of forgiveness
to all who draw near
recognizing their sin.
With an open, loving heart,
you acknowledge our fidelity
even in the little we have done,
and give us new opportunities
to be good and faithful servants
in the much that still needs to be done. Amen.

Ecumenical Advocacy Alliance

Jesus, Son of God, Son of man and woman,
you taught us well.
You showed us how to live.
And yet. And yet.
We falter.
Deny injustice, hurt instead of heal,
use hands as weapons.
Choose faithlessness instead of loyalty.
Choose security instead of risk.
Smile instead of weep.
Choose indifference in the face of violence.
Jesus, Son of God,
Forgive us for we know not what we do. Amen.

PACSA

Merciful God,
We meet each other today at this cross,
    members of your broken body, the Church,
    citizens of . . . . ,
    inhabitants of one world . . . .

As those who inflict wounds on each other:
be merciful to us.
As those who deny justice to others:
be merciful to us.
As those who are greedy:
be merciful to us.
As those who are blind to the poverty around us:
be merciful to us.
As those who put people living with HIV on trial:
be merciful to us.
As those who discriminate based on our own race or culture or
    gender:
be merciful to us.
As those who are deaf to the cries of the traumatized:
be merciful to us.
As those who seek to use power to control others:
be merciful to us.
As those who refuse to receive:
be merciful to us.
As those afraid of this world's torment:
be merciful to us.

Giver of life,
we wait with you
to bear your hope to earth's darkest places.

Where love is denied:
let love break through.
Where justice is destroyed:
let righteousness rule.
Where hope is crucified:
let faith persist.
Where peace is no more:
let passion live on.
Where truth is denied
let the struggle continue.

Merciful God,
as we accept your assurance of forgiveness
let us know once more the dawn of life
that we may bring hope to the hopeless,
courage to the fearful
and peace to those in distress,
through your Son, our Saviour, Jesus Christ,
who was crucified
and who rose again,
our Lord and our God.
Amen.

Diakonia Council of Churches, South Africa

O God,
whose longing is to reconcile the whole universe within your love,
pour out your abundant mercy on your Church,
and on your world so fragmented and torn apart.

For the history of pain and travail,
oppression and prejudice inflicted on women,
within the Church and in the world,

O God, forgive us and pour out your mercy.

For our failure to resist the bitterness
which poisons and sours the gospel of love and reconciliation,

O God, forgive us and pour out your mercy.

For our failure to present a wounded world with hope for
    reconciliation
within a true and loving community of men and women,

O God, forgive us and pour out your mercy.

O God,
whose longing is to reconcile the whole universe within your love,
pour out your abundant mercy on your Church
and your world so fragmented and torn apart:
this we plead through the love of Jesus Christ.
Amen.

PASCA

God of peace,
forgive us
for fuelling anger,
for harbouring vengeance,
and not heeding your call to love one another.
Inspire us
to hold on to hope,
to hold fast to courage,
and to live for the day when there shall be peace.
Amen.

Christian Aid (adapted)

O Christ,
in whose body was named
all the violence of the world,
and in whose memory is contained
our profoundest grief.

We lay open to you:
the violence done in our name in time before memory;
the unremembered wounds we have inflicted;
the injuries we cannot forget and for which we have not been
    forgiven.

The remembrance of them is grievous to us;
the burden of them is intolerable.

We lay open to you:
The victims of violence whose only memorial is our anger;
Those whose suffering was sustained on our behalf;
Those whose continued oppression provides the ground we stand on.

The remembrance of them is grievous to us;
the burden of them is intolerable.

We wholeheartedly repent
of the evil we have done,
and of the evil done on our behalf;
and we look for grace to offer forgiveness
and to know ourselves forgiven.

PASCA

Search me, O God, and know my heart;
test me, and know my thoughts.
See if there is any wicked in me,
and lead in the way everlasting.
Amen.
(Psalm 139.23–24)

Methodist Church, South Africa

O Christ for whom we search,
our help when help has failed:
give us courage to expose our need
and ask to be made whole;
that, being touched by you,
we may be raised to new life
in the power of your name. Amen.

Diakonia Council of Churches, South Africa

God of healing,
bless us and heal us
from our self-preoccupation,
from our cynicism and apathy,
from all that disables us
in the face of the need to change and be changed.
Touch us so that we are empowered to go out and touch others.
Amen.

Christian Aid

PRAYERS AND COLLECTS

May none of God's wonderful works keep silence,
night or morning,
bright stars, high mountains,
the depths of the seas, the springs of rushing rivers;
may all these break into song
as we sing to Father, Son and Holy Spirit.
May all the angels in the heavens reply
'Amen, Amen, Amen'.
Power, praise, honour, eternal glory

to God, the only giver of grace.
Amen, Amen, Amen.

North African monastic community, 3rd century

Spirit of Life in the dust and the sunshine,
Spirit of Life in sickness and laughter,
Spirit of Life in friendship and grieving,
Spirit of Life for workers and traders,
Spirit of Life for campaigners and givers.
The Spirit of Life is God's gift to the world.
Amen.

Christian Aid

We stand side-by-side:
collectors and givers,
those who pray and those who campaign,
rich and poor united in God,
longing for justice and living in joy,
together we pray:
Holy Spirit of God,
light a flame with me,
burning for justice,
glowing with kindness,
shining with hope
for the end of poverty
and the peace of all people
in this ever-turning world. Amen.

Christian Aid

Underneath me are two feet –
please may they do the task willingly;
in front of me are rows of doors –
please may they open to me cheerfully;
in my hand are dozens of envelopes –
please may they be filled generously;
in my heart are millions of needy people –
may all I do this week make this
a world in which they can thrive.

Christian Aid

O God, you have prepared in peace the path I am walking today.
Help me to walk straight on that path.
When I speak, remove lies from my mouth.
If I am hungry, take away from me all complaint.
If I have plenty, destroy pride in me.
May I continue through this day calling on you –
you, O Lord, who know no other Lord.
Amen.

Traditional Ethiopian

Grant, O God, your protection;
and in your protection, strength and understanding;
and in understanding, knowledge;
and in knowledge, the knowledge of justice;
and in the knowledge of justice, the love of it;
and in that love, the love of life;
and in the love of life, the love of God:
God in all goodness.
Amen.

Methodist Church, South Africa

Almighty God, our heavenly Father, the privilege is ours to share in
the loving, healing, reconciling mission of your son, Jesus Christ, our
Lord, in this age and wherever we are. For without you we can do no
good thing:
    may your Spirit make us wise;
    may your Spirit guide us;
    may your Spirit renew us and
    may your Spirit strengthen us
so that we will be:
    strong in faith;
    discerning in proclamation;
    courageous in witness and
    persistent in good deeds.
This we ask through the name of the one who created us.
    Amen.

Church of the Province, West Indies

God of abundance,
we give thanks for the harvest;
the harvest of agriculture,
the harvest of education,
the harvest of justice.
May abundant and joyful harvests
be found in all the lands of the world.
Amen.

Christian Aid

Generous God,
in you we see lavish abundance.
Remind us of your glory and generosity
as we encounter the needs and shortages of the world.
Work through us to share your generosity
so that all the world may come to share in celebration.
Amen.

Christian Aid

Gracious Lord,
We give you our will,
    as Mary gave.
We give you our worship,
    as the shepherds gave.
We give you our riches,
    as the wise men gave.
We give you our lives,
    as you gave your life for us.
In Jesus' name, Amen.

Christian Aid

Women of Ethiopia

Like a mother
who wraps
a beloved child to her back,
intimate, yet other,
bound, yet free
to give and to receive,
to hold and to release,

you bear us, Lord.

Like the woman
bent double
under her cross-shaped load –
sweet smelling, bitter bundle –
dead weight, living light,
ensuring today's bread,
tomorrow's hope,

you deliver us, Lord.

Like the dawn women
who daily greet
the rising sun,
white-robed lilies of the field,
wearing Sheba's beauty and Solomon's pride,
responding to faith's ancient call
to be one with you in Spirit,

you love us, Lord.

Annabel Shilson-Thomas

Subversive God,
remind us when we hear your story
that it is rarely those in positions of power and influence
who can show us where you are.
Rather,
it is in the company of children, the poor and the marginalized
that we shall discover your presence –
there we shall find you.

Christian Aid (adapted)

Love incarnate –
you changed our world forever.
You dwelt with the poor
and raised the humble high.

Love come in –
change our hearts,
Challenge our consumerism
and fill us with your love.

Love reach out –
change our world forever.
Bring life to the poor
and freedom to the oppressed.

In your precious name, Jesus.
Amen.

Christian Aid

As I enter the street market,
wheel my trolley at the superstore,
leaf through a catalogue or log on to the internet:
be with me and help me
when I spend my money.
Be with me and help me
to see the market place as you see it –
as wide as the world you love so much.
Be with us and help us
to share the markets we share
for all people.
As we live under your steady gaze,
so we can change, by your gracious love.
Amen.

Christian Aid

Gracious Father,
who sent your Holy Spirit
so that all the world might know the goodness of God;
grant us such gifts as we need
to seek good news for the poor,
peace for those who live in fear,
and justice for all people;
through our Lord Jesus Christ,
who is alive and reigns with you,
in the unity of the Holy Spirit,
one God, now and forever.
Amen.

Christian Aid

Creator God,
you loved the world into life.
Forgive us when our dreams of the future
are shaped by anything other than glimpses of a kingdom
of justice, peace and an end to poverty.

Incarnate God,
you taught us to speak out for what is right.
Make us content with nothing less than a world
that is transformed into the shape of love,
where poverty shall be no more.

Breath of God,
let there be abundant life.
Inspire us with a vision of a changed world
where poverty is no more,
and give us the faith, courage and will to make it happen.

Christian Aid

Lord, you placed us in the world to be its salt.
Give us the vision
to preserve the good of your creation
and give us the courage to be the salt in the wounds of the world,
to cleanse corruption and injustice
and to bring healing and relief to those who suffer.
Amen.

Christian Aid

'Someone's crying Lord'

In the following prayer, everyone sings the refrain, then a small group sings again softly while the verse is read.

Kumba Yah, my Lord, Kumba Yah (x3)
O Lord, Kumba Yah.

Someone's crying Lord, Kumba Yah (x3)
O Lord, Kumba Yah.

Someone's crying Lord.
That 'someone' is not one,

but several million, Lord,
some men but mostly women.
Theirs are tears of fear and suffering.
Theirs are tears of strength and resistance.
Theirs are tears of weakness and disappointment.
Women are crying, Lord, redeem the times.

Someone's dying, Lord . . . (x3)

Someone's dying of hunger and thirst.
Not one, but many,
because structures and systems
crush the poor and alienate the rich.
Someone's dying, Lord,
because we are not prepared to take sides,
to make a choice and witness to your call.
Women are dying, Lord,
Redeem our structures and our systems.

Someone's shouting, Lord . . . (x3)

Someone's shouting, Lord,
shouting out boldly with courage.
Someone has made a choice,
is ready to challenge oppression,
with confidence and commitment,
is ready to fight against the evils
that crucify each other.
Someone's shouting, Lord.
Redeem her and strengthen her hands.

Someone's praying, Lord . . . (x3)

Someone's praying, Lord.
We pray with them
in frustration and weakness,
strength and endurance;
We are praying, Lord.
Spur our imagination, sharpen our will,
Touch us to be touched,
Bless us to be a blessing.
We are praying, Lord,
Renew and transform the times.

Kumba Yah, my Lord, Kumba Yah . . . (x3)
O Lord, Kumba Yah.

Asian women doing Theology, Hong Kong

We pray for all women and children living with HIV and AIDS.
In their pain, deliver them,
In their wondering why, give them courage
And in their coping, give them strength.
We give thanks for the lives of those we have lost.
In our sorrow, comfort us,
In our emptiness, sustain us
And in our fear, relieve us.
Amen.

Diakona Council of Churches, South Africa

Dear God,
friends with AIDS slip through my fingers
faster than grains of sand, and seemingly as many.
I can't hold them.

God, dear God,
please catch them with your open hands,
within your welcoming embrace,
with your loving heart.

I wish I could be there for them.
I pray they'll be there for me
when I slip.
You too, my God,
Our God.
Amen.

Diakona Council of Churches, South Africa

Holy God,
you breathe your life into each child born,
willing them to grow into all fullness.
Yet we allow your children to go hungry for lack of bread,
to wander homeless for lack of care,

to be violated for lack of protection,
to go sick for lack of medicine,
to die for lack of life.

Holy Jesus,
Forgive us for our blindness and lack of love;
Forgive us for our failure to provide
    your bread,
    your care,
    your protection,
    your healing
    and your life.

Holy Spirit,
Help us to work for a world
    where each child is valued and knows their worth,
    where tears turn to laughter and despair to joy
    and where we see in each child the image of God.
Amen.

Diakonia Council of Churches, South Africa

God of all the world,
give us wisdom in troubled times.
As we realize how fragile our systems of security are,
remind us how much more fragile they are for those who have
    nothing.
As we talk of financial crisis,
remind us of those who go to bed hungry.
As we face challenges over our own resources,
remind us to share what we have.
As we fear doing without,
remind us to live in a Christ-like way
and bring peace to a world in turmoil.
Amen.

Christian Aid (adapted)

Compassionate God,
Give us the strength to enact your love when tragedy strikes,
and the imagination to grieve with those who mourn.
For when we mourn, we respond in love;
When we respond in love, we respond in your name;
and when we respond in your name,
We believe that new life and hope is possible.
Amen.

Christian Aid (adapted)

Hear me, Jesus, hear me!
Listen to the words I pray.
This is what your children ask:
For peace and happiness in . . .

Christian Aid

Praise our God, O peoples.
Let the sound of his praise be heard.
For he has preserved our lives.
He has kept our feet from slipping.
We went through fire and water,
But you brought us to a place of abundance.
Come and listen, all you who fear God;
Shout to all the world of the good that he has done.
I will praise God in his holy temple.
My worship will be kindled like fire.
God has surely listened and heard my humble voice.
Praise be to God, who has not rejected my prayer.

Psalm 66.8–20

PRAYERS OF COMMITMENT

God of power,
God of people,
you are the life of all that lives,
energy that fills the earth,
vitality that brings to birth,

the impetus toward making whole
whatever is bruised or broken.
In you, we grow to know the truth
that sets all creation free.
You are the song the whole earth sings,
the promise liberation brings,
now and forever.

We commit ourselves anew to your work in the world
as you come to meet us
with the promise of hope and strength.

Diakona Council of Churches, South Africa

God of the impossible,
we pray for justice, peace and reconciliation;
when the challenges seem too many,
remind us of your resurrection power;
when the task seems overwhelming,
remind us of the miracle of love;
and when apathy threatens us,
remind us of your vision of a world made whole.
Help us to hope that the impossible can happen
and live as if it might do so today.
Amen.

Christian Aid (adapted)

After the rain,
let there be rebuilding;
after the violence,
let there be reconciliation;
after the suffering,
let there be restoration.
After others have forgotten,
let me be one who remembers.
Amen.

Christian Aid

As I drink my coffee,
I think of the hands that tended the beans,
the hands that harvested the crop,
the hands that paid for it and took it,
the hands that loaded it onto a ship to bring it halfway across the
    world,
the hands that operated the machines that roasted it and processed it,
the hands that put it onto the supermarket shelf,
the hands that hesitate in front of a bewildering choice of brands,
and my hands, cradled round a cup.

Christian Aid

God of infinite wisdom and grace,
    you hold all people in your hands.
In response to the life you bring
    through the suffering and resurrection of your Son Jesus,
we commit ourselves to work for a more just society,
    where the structures of poverty will be understood and challenged,
    where those suffering in body or mind will be accepted and healed,
    where all people will love each other as equally created in your
    image,
    where powerlessness will be changed to strength
    and where the rights and responsibilities of all will be defended.
We commit ourselves
    to bring peace where there is conflict,
    to bring healing where there is suffering,
    to bring light where there is darkness,
    to bring hope where there is despair,
    to bring life where there is death,
through the power of the cross of Jesus,
    his glorious resurrection,
    and the mighty outpouring of the Holy Spirit.
    Amen.

Diakonia Council of Churches, South Africa

Group 1 We believe that beyond the violence,
Group 2 there can be love;
Group 1 that beyond the despair,
Group 2 there can be hope;
Group 1 that beyond the torment,
Group 2 we will find rest;
Group 1 that beyond our brokenness,
Group 2 there can be healing;
Group 1 that beyond our agony,
Group 2 we will find joy.
All   Oh, God, transform our disbelief
and gently carry us from darkness to light.

PACSA

Lord God, give us the spirit of courage
that we may be open in our concern for our neighbour,
give us the spirit of challenge
that we may not accept silence and prejudice without question,
give us the spirit of compassion
that we may see the world through their eyes,
give us the spirit of gentleness
that we may listen to those who cry out to us for understanding,
give us the spirit of togetherness
that we may truly love one another as ourselves.
Lord God, with the help and guidance of your Holy Spirit,
lead us forward, in the name of your Son, Jesus Christ, we pray.
Amen.

Diakona Council of Churches, South Africa

We reject all forms of discrimination and stigma,
   because we believe in God,
     who created the world in all its diversity and colour,
     HIV positive and negative alike.
We honour the dignity of all people,
   because we believe in Jesus Christ,
     who took upon himself the pain and suffering of the world,
     carers and sufferers alike.
We speak and act with one prophetic voice,

because we believe in the Holy Spirit,
who summons us out of our complacency,
voiceless and influential alike.
And we call upon governments to honour their commitments of funds
and services in the fight against HIV,
as we stand as one with those who live in the shadow of HIV,
for the eyes of the Lord are on us all.
Amen.

Diakona Council of Churches, South Africa

INTERCESSIONS

Leader In gratitude to God, in whom we live and move and exist,
let us remember all men and women of good will, who strive
for the good they know, who love their neighbours and are
willing to work and suffer for truth, justice, peace and love.

All   **Giver of life, breath and bread, Creator of every race, we
will take our stand with all who see something of your
truth, and live for it.**

Leader In sorrow and in hope, let us remember the evil of the world;
the illness and sorrow which we cannot avoid; the fear and
the loneliness which we ourselves create; the poverty and
hunger toward which we contribute by our selfishness; our
destruction of nature and of each other; the injustice, oppression and war, which are always with us.

All   **God, we are all your children. We will meet our neighbours'
needs, proclaim your loving purpose and follow Christ
through death to resurrection.**

Leader Let us praise God. He has given us life, purpose within that
life, and hope that the purpose will be fulfilled.

All   **Lord, our Lord, your name is the greatest in the world!
Lord, our Lord, your name is the greatest in the world.
Amen.**

Diakonia Council of Churches, South Africa

Leader   We pray for poor people, scarred by war and impoverished by financial systems over which they have no control. That such poverty might end, that the wealth of the few might be redistributed for the welfare of the many and that every nation may determine its own future, we pray:
          Your kingdom come,
All   **Your will be done.**

Leader   We pray for people who are marginalized and exploited, who put themselves in danger in order that they and their families might survive. That such exploitation might end, and that all may have the opportunity to earn a decent living, we pray:
          Your kingdom come,
All   **Your will be done.**

Leader   We pray for children and teenagers in developing countries whose horizons are limited, who do the work of adults and dare not dream for fear of disappointment. That children's education and health may be secure, that their potential may be fulfilled, that they might be given visions of a better future and the energy to reshape nations, we pray:
          Your kingdom come,
All   **Your will be done.**

Christian Aid

Leader   God our Father, we thank you that you have made each one of us in your own image and given us gifts and talents with which to serve you. We thank you for those whose lives we have shared and whom we remember now. We thank you for the good we have experienced in them and for the blessing they have been to us. Give us faith to leave them in your care, confident in your promises.

Leader   We live in much darkness. We are often uncertain. We are sometimes afraid.
All   **In the darkness, we light a candle of hope.**

First candle is lit.

Leader   We all have sorrows. We have known pain. Each of us carries special regrets.

All   **In our palm, we light a candle of forgiveness.**

Second candle is lit.

Leader   We are sometimes lonely, and the world seems cold and hard.

All   **In our loneliness, we light a candle of love.**

Third candle is lit.

Leader   We have known awe, wonder, mystery and glimmerings of perfection in our imperfect world.

All   **In our wonder, we light a candle of praise.**

Fourth candle is lit.

Leader   May our separate lights become one flame, that together we may be nourished by its glow.

Diakonia Council of Churches, South Africa

Leader   For children who suffer pain and degradation, and rejection by those responsible for their care:

All   **Merciful God, grant them safety and protection.**

Leader   For mothers and fathers who suffer the anguish of their failure as parents:

All   **Merciful God, grant them insight and healing.**

Leader   For women who are abused and battered by those who profess to love them:

All   **Merciful God, grant them strength and courage.**

Leader   For men who batter those they love:

All   **Merciful God, grant them true repentance and the heart to change.**

Leader   For all Christians:

All   **Merciful God, grant them understanding and compassion for the suffering of others.**

Leader God of love, restore all families to your loving care. Give them inner strength and patient wisdom to overcome arrogance and division. May they resolve conflict without violence, and nurture one another in the spirit of the love and peace proclaimed by Jesus our Lord.

All **Amen.**

PACSA

Leader Our God, heal us from social structures that condemn many to poverty and ill-health.

All **Heal us in your grace, and transform this world.**

Leader Our God, heal us from unfair international trade and exploitative economic policies.

All **Heal us in your grace, and transform this world.**

Leader Our God, heal us from exploitative relationships that expose women to HIV infection and disease.

All **Heal us in your grace, and transform this world.**

Leader Our God, heal us from unhealthy family relationships that bring pain and hurt.

All **Heal us in your grace, and transform this world.**

Leader Our God, heal us from the prejudice that isolates those most vulnerable and the discrimination that prevents access to care.

All **Heal us in your grace, and transform this world.**

Leader Our God, heal us from resignation and exhaustion that make us inactive and blind to the fullness of life.

All **Heal us in your grace, and transform this world.**

Leader Our God, heal us from grief that breaks our spirits and leave us empty.

All **Heal us in your grace, and transform this world.**
Heal us with your resurrection power.
Cause us to rise from fear and hopelessness.
Cause us to rise into your resurrection hope.
Cause us to claim our right to life and quality of life.
Transform us through the joy of your spirit

and your peace that surpasses all our understanding.
Amen.

Adapted from South African Council of Churches

Leader   We are all affected by HIV and AIDS.
All   **We are the body of Christ.**

Leader   We have lost close relatives.
All   **Heal our bodies.**

Leader   We have lost close friends and neighbours;
All   **Heal our hearts.**

Leader   We have lost church and work mates.
All   **Heal our spirits.**

Leader   We have lost our hope
All   **Heal our minds.**

Leader   We put our trust in you,
All   **You are Emmanuel, God with us.**
   You will never leave us or forsake us.
   You will be with us to the end of the ages.
   Amen.

Diakonia Council of Churches, South Africa

Leader   Loving God,
   As we hold before you a world confronted by AIDS,
   we pray in hope for your will to prevail:

Leader   Where lives are short,
All   **may they yet be full.**

Leader   When a cure is far off,
All   **may there yet be healing.**

Leader   Where bodies are weak,
All   **may spirits yet be strong.**

Leader   When silence is destructive,
All   **may there yet be courage to speak out.**

Leader	Where judgments are hasty,
All	**may minds yet be open.**

Leader	When reality is overwhelming,
All	**may there yet be response.**

Leader	Where faith is tested,
All	**may we yet find you there.**

Leader	In the name of Jesus,
All	**Amen.**

Diakonia Council of Churches, South Africa

BLESSINGS

The blessing of our gracious God,
the blessing of our risen Jesus,
the blessing of our life-giving Spirit,
be on all that is good in God's creation,
seen and unseen,
evermore.
Amen.

Christian Aid

May God the Father bless us with hearts of compassion;
may Jesus Christ bless us with a vision of a world transformed;
may the Holy Spirit bless us with gifts to use in God's service;
and so may each of us rejoice to know the goodness of the Lord,
now and evermore. Amen.

Christian Aid

May the God of the poor challenge us to work for justice.
May Christ our deliverer give us hope for the future.
May the Spirit of truth shine in our darkness and bring us peace.
And may the blessing of God,
Creator, Redeemer and Sustainer,
be with us all, now and for evermore. Amen.

Diakonia Council of Churches, South Africa

May Christ who healed the bent-over woman
   heal your pain;

May Christ who told the daughters of Jerusalem
   to weep not for him but for themselves and their children
     welcome you and dry your tears;

May Christ who hung alone on the cross,
   deserted by all but a few faithful women,
     stand alongside you in your suffering;

May Christ who rose from the dead
   And appeared first to Mary Magdalene
     Raise you and send you out to proclaim your story.

In the name of God,
   Creator, Redeemer, Sustainer,
     our memory, authority and hope of the future.
Amen.

Source unknown

May God, our loving Parent, bless you
and fill you with compassion, tenderness and love
for the children of the world.

May Christ, our Saviour, bless you
and strengthen you to denounce abuse and violence
against the children of the world.

May the warm, brooding Spirit, bless you
and send you out to work for a world
where every child is protected and cherished.

In the name of the Holy Trinity, Amen.

Diakonia Council of Churches, South Africa

May the blessing of the God of peace and justice be with us;
May the blessing of the Son who weeps the tears of those who suffer
   be with us;
And may the blessing of the Spirit who inspires us to reconciliation
   and hope be with us; from now into eternity.
Amen.

South Africa Council of Churches

Go out into the world and take with you,
the hope of God our creator who in love
created a world where all would be whole
and longs for that wholeness to be restored,
the hope of Jesus who touched and ate with the broken
and offered them healing as he offers us now,
the hope of the Spirit who inspires and guides and energizes
us in times of apathy and despair
to work to bring all God's people into oneness and health.
Amen.

Diakonia Council of Churches, South Africa

Lord bless us,
in our work and in our rest,
in our campaigning and in our praying,
in our church and in your world.
Let us go out from this place
sure in the knowledge that
with you all things are possible.
Let us go out from this place
faithfully believing that
you will make all things new.
Amen.

Christian Aid

May the Lord watch over you;
May he prevent your foot from slipping on the journey;
May the Lord be the shade at your right hand;
May the Lord keep you from all harm;
May he watch over your life;
May the Lord watch over your coming and going
both now and for evermore. Amen.

Celtic blessing

A blessing on the men and on the women;
A blessing on our sleep and on our rising;
A blessing on the rich and on the poor;
A blessing on all who cry out to Jesus.
This night and ever more. Amen.

Christian Aid

In our living and loving,
The blessing of God.
In singing and praying,
The blessing of God.
In giving and acting,
The blessing of God.
In strength and in vulnerability,
The blessing of God.
In seeking justice and peace,
The blessing of God.
On our brothers and sisters throughout the world,
The blessing of God.
This day and every day,
Amen.

Christian Aid

SENDING OUT

Loving God,
you call us
to follow where you lead
to live as you live,
to love as you love.
Give us the courage to walk the way of the cross
to listen to your voice
to speak your word
and empower us to be co-creators
in building your kingdom of justice and peace.
Amen

Christian Aid (adapted)

Walk with those who stumble,
Stand with those who fall,
Weep with those who grieve,
Feel for those who mourn.
Stay awake with those who cannot sleep,
Sit with those who cannot weep,
Listen to those who need to speak,
Speak with those who need to hear.
Reach out to those who hide,
Hold hands with the despised.
Understand the fearful,
Calm the anxious,
Reconcile the angry,
Bring peace to the troubled.
Sing
Dance
Rejoice
Laugh
Smile
Love all God's creation people,
Let God's kingdom come!

Adaption by Annabel Shilson-Thomas

Part Three

Biblical Reflections and Stories of Change

Biblical Reflections

This chapter contains a variety of biblical reflections of different styles that can be used by groups, for personal reflection or as an aid to sermon preparation.

BEING ONE BODY

This interactive reflection looks at what it feels like to be excluded. Originally it was used to challenge the marginalization of people living with HIV in South Africa, but it has been adapted so that it can be used to explore what it feels like to feel excluded in any setting, and to emphasize the inclusive nature of God's kingdom.

Reading: 1 Corinthians 13.12–27

Reflection: Being the body of Christ

Leader   What you do to another, you do to yourself and to all of
          us.
          In the deepest sense, we are one person, a universal body.
          When we destroy another person, we also destroy some-
          thing within ourselves, and as a consequence, something in
          humanity. But this does not mean that we are all alike. There
          is great diversity among us, in the same way that diversity
          exists within each and every one of us.

Complainers 1 and 2 are at the back of the worship area.

All   'How long, O Lord? Will you forget me forever?'

Complainer 1   'It is as though people avoid me, talk behind my back, they treat me like I'm different. They think of me as being a loser, I'm excluded.'

Complainer 2   'I don't dare tell anyone that I'm . . . ., because I don't know how others will react.'

Complainer 1   'I'm so sick and tired of all the questions! I have needs too . . .'

Complainer 2   'Some people see only my disability/my illness/my gender/my sexuality/my colour/my size; they don't see me!'

Complainer 1   'I'm so afraid of being rejected or disappointed.'

Complainer 2   'Why does it seem like God is angry when I try to do my best?'

Complainer 1   'I have searched for a God who loves me, who doesn't judge and who can help me to accept myself. I didn't find him in the church. It has been a lonesome search.'

All   **'How long, O Lord? Will you forget me forever?'**

Confession of our participation in what is constructive

From the front of the worship area:

Reader 1   We confess that we are a part of all that God has created and he saw that it was 'very good', that we all have a part in the good and bear within ourselves a basic goodness.

We confess that all our being, also our physical body, our longings and desires are all a part of God's image within us.

We confess that we all have value, and that we have value because we are God's creation, because we live and exist.

Silence

Acknowledgment of our participation in what is destructive

From either side of the front of the worship area:

Reader 2 We acknowledge our part in creating divisions and placing some people on the outside.

We acknowledge our prejudices, that we fear what is foreign to us and that we contribute to people's feelings of isolation, being shunned and treated as though they were different.

We acknowledge that we are often more concerned about a person's status and their being different than we are about their inner resources, potential and common humanity.

We acknowledge that we often identify certain people or groups of people as being bad, and that we do not see that we are all a part of what is evil as well as what is good.

We acknowledge injustice in that the strongest, the healthiest and the wealthiest among us are often prioritized, receive the best and in that way receive even more.

Look upon us in mercy, forgive us, cleanse us and make us whole.

Silence

Absolution

Leader You are loved, far more than you know – loved, forgiven and redeemed.

And this love sustains your life. Your deepest identity IS love.

STEWARDSHIP OF CREATION

This reflection looks at what it means to be stewards of God's creation and how it affects our relationship not just with the earth but also with our global neighbours.

Readings

Genesis 1.27–31 and 2.15–17: God entrusts Adam and Eve with creation

Psalm 8: Praise for God's creation, and the wonder of it being entrusted to humankind.

Matthew 20.20–27: Jesus explains leadership modelled on service.

Reflection: God entrusts Adam and Eve with creation

The first chapter of Genesis tells us of God's joy in creation. In chapter 1, verse 26, God gives men and women creation to enjoy. Note the order in which this happens – God creates the world and then creates humans. He does not create the world for humans. In Genesis 2:15 God states that Adam and Eve must care for the garden, a responsibility that the writer of Psalm 8 recognizes as being an incredible privilege for humankind.

Adam and Eve are given the garden to enjoy and nurture; not to take from it at will. Instead of being given scope to expect, demand and exploit, everything is within their maker's jurisdiction. This 'care-taking' approach to creation is extended to people in the New Testament. Jesus' teachings are clear on the responsibility that comes with any form of leadership or power. Christ not only cared for the poor and humble, but demonstrated qualities of personal service towards them, in complete contrast to expectation and prevailing attitudes and behaviour. He redefined power as protection, leadership as service, and privileges as responsibilities. In Matthew 20:27, he urges us to do the same.

Responsibilities or selfish demands?

Adam and Eve forget that the garden has been entrusted to them as a responsibility. They sin because they set themselves up as equal to God; they take what they decide is theirs to subdue and dominate. In many of our activities, both individually and corporately, we do the same. We forget that God's world is a gift that carries responsibility. Instead, we view the world's resources as our own, and exploit them for our own gain. When our thinking strays away from God's 'care-taking' charge, and into a 'taking' outlook, we fail to do God's will for the world. We adopt lifestyles and systems which perpetuate our wealth, and exploit the poor.

Restoring God's priorities

We need to recognize how dependent we are on God's creation, and to give thanks for its incredible richness and diversity, resolving to pray and campaign for a change to exploitative systems. Let us commit to using our prosperity and influence to take care of the world's resources and to serve those who have so little.

SHARING OUR HARVEST

While this short reflection focuses on harvest, it asks us to think about the nature and content of our celebrations. What does it mean to celebrate while others go hungry? It challenges us to see our celebrations as an opportunity to give, for if we fail to share with others our worship is hollow.

Readings

Psalm 126: Those who sow in tears will reap with songs of joy.

Isaiah 58.6–7: Is not this the fast I have chosen: to loose the chains of injustice . . .?

James 1.27: Religion . . . is . . . to look after orphans and widows in their distress.

Matthew 25.31–46: Whatever you do to the least of these you do to me.

Reflection: Harvest is a celebration

Harvest is a celebration to thank God for our food. It is also a time to celebrate with others. We are encouraged by seeing God's promise fulfilled, or in the words of Psalm 126, seeds sown with weeping have turned to harvests reaped with joy. But what about those for whom harvest yields no joy?

Harvest is also a time of mourning

One of the hardest things about celebrating harvest is the hunger we see. Why doesn't God always turn weeping into joy? We may not be able to answer this question directly. But in Matthew 25 we are given a precious insight. There is enough for everyone, if it is shared; if those with more than enough recognize their calling to give and enact justice. Hearts moved by the Spirit to choose to give reveal God's sacrificial love. By learning how blessed it is to give, we can complete the harvest as we share with others. Harvest is a time to stand in solidarity with those who have nothing, and to pray and act for a transformed world.

What is Jesus saying about the poor?

Jesus' words must have sounded preposterous to his hearers, who lived in a society that ostracized the poor, who were deemed out of reach of God's favour, as sin and poverty were connected in many strands of Jewish thinking; so equating the poor and downtrodden with God was shocking, particularly as Jesus includes the stranger or alien, who was considered totally beyond God's care. Jesus makes it clear that the 'least of these' are made in God's image; and even suggests that this is where we should start if we are looking for God.

What is Jesus saying about worship?

Echoing scriptures such as Isaiah 58 and James 1.27, worship is not just about acts of piety or following the letter of the law. Real worship is a natural outpouring of what God has shown them; an outpouring of their very selves. When we give sacrificially we are praising God without even knowing it, and helping God's kingdom to be realized now. Thereby, mourning can be turned to celebration and our harvest celebrations are not hollow.

GOD'S BIAS

This short reflection, which could be used for the basis of a sermon or bible study, invites us to think about what we understand by 'fairness' and challenges us beyond the notion of what's fair to what God requires of us: the same extravagant love for others as he shows to us.

Readings

Matthew 10.1–16: The parable of the Workers in the Vineyard

See also
Luke 6.20–36: The Beatitudes
Matthew 5.1–12: The Beatitudes
Luke 10.25–37: The parable of the Good Samaritan
Luke 15.11–31: The parable of the Prodigal Son

Reflection: Fairness or favour?

The Bible is full of examples of unfairness, of stories of God treating people unfairly. But this is treating 'fairness' as being the same as 'equal'. God doesn't tell us to treat people equally. In so many things that God did, he favoured the poorest people, the outcast and the hated enemies.

And in so many parables and metaphors of the kingdom of God, Jesus describes God as not only treating people unfairly, but also being abundantly, extravagantly unfair; and abundantly and extravagantly generous. This is God's grace – giving us not what we deserve but blessings far beyond what we could ever earn or deserve.

Contrast this with the way the human race treats each other. How rich countries treat poor countries. How wealthy and powerful people treat the poor and powerless. At best, it is grudgingly an agreed minimum standard. We have set ourselves minimum standards for children's rights through the UN Declaration of the Rights of the Child; and some very low targets for how we are going to tackle poverty through the millennium development goals. And it seems to some people that we're not even working very hard at those.

We're not even reaching fairness, let alone what God has in mind, which is an abundant love that doesn't count the cost, an indiscriminate love for all people.

God doesn't want us to be fair, to treat people equally. God wants us to favour the poor, the forgotten, those others reject. We're called to be biased, partisan, unreasonably generous.

In 2008, governments in rich countries gave ten times more help to struggling banks than they had given in the last ten years to poor countries struggling with their international debts. That's quite the opposite – being biased against the poor and favouring ourselves.

HEARING THE BIBLE THROUGH OTHER PEOPLE'S EARS

All scripture was given in a particular context. The Bible records God's dealing with humanity in many different situations for over a thousand years. We normally hear the words of scripture in our own context, which for us is reasonably comfortable. But these reflections invite us to imagine we're hearing the Bible as people from El Salvador. While designed for groups, they could provide the basis for a talk or sermon.

Reflection: Listening as if we are . . .

Leader   Let all the men listen as if they were:

Voice 1   Joaquin (*Ho-ak-een*) Duran Bermudez, a 66-year-old man who in the 1980s was conscripted into the National Guard to fight against his fellow countrymen. Joaquin lost a leg and supplements his small pension by growing corn. This is not a commercial enterprise, as Salvadorean corn is undercut by corn imported from Mexico by large food companies. And each year he risks losing everything to heavy rains, tropical storms or even hurricanes.

Leader   And let all the women listen as if they were:

Voice 2   Elisabeth (*E-leessa-bet*), a 44-year-old woman, abandoned by her husband, who is the sole wage earner for her four children and her mother. With no welfare system, no education or skills, and poverty all around, the only way she can earn sufficient money is to be a part-time sex worker, at daily risk of abuse.

Leader   And let all the young people listen as if they were:

Voice 3   Jesús (*Heh-soos*) Antonio Echevarria (or 'Chus' for short), a 15-year-old boy whose father is dead and whose mother, an alcoholic, only visits him occasionally. Until recently his community had no running water. Chus gets up at 6 am, makes his own breakfast and spends half the day at school, for which he has to buy all the books, and half the day fishing with his brother-in-law. He lives in a hut with holes in the roof and hens and chickens under his bed.

Leader   So now let us hear two passages of scripture, written to two
          different communities almost 700 years apart. Let us hear
          them as if we were Joaquin or Elisabeth or Chus, and let us
          ask ourselves which portion of the Bible would give us more
          hope.

Readings

Amos 5.7–14
Ephesians 6.1–3, 5–8

Group reflection

1 Discuss with the person next to you which reading you found more
  helpful for your character, and why. The leader may ask one or two
  people to explain their choice.
2 Reflect on why it is that the same passage of scripture may for us be a
  challenge to our comfortable lifestyle, whereas for people who know
  poverty and persecution, the same words may speak of the promise
  of God.
3 Read Psalm 94 and think about why it is sung so enthusiastically in
  El Salvador.

GENDER AND POWER

This reflection invites us to look afresh at the well-known story of Jairus' daughter and the woman with a haemorrhage, and to explore the
issue of power and empowerment, and how it relates to gender.

Reading

Mark 5.21–43: Jairus' daughter and the woman with a haemorrhage

Reflection: Empowering others

In the gospel story, Jairus, leader of the synagogue, came to Jesus, fell
at his feet and begged him repeatedly saying, 'My daughter is at the
point of death. Come lay your hands on her so that she may be made
well and live.' Jesus agreed to come along with Jairus and a big crowd
followed.

The story also tells us that there was a woman who had been suffering from haemorrhages for 12 years. This woman had 'endured much under many physicians and had spent all that she had; and she was no better, but rather she grew worse.' But when she heard about Jesus, she said to herself: 'If I but touch his clothes, I will be made well.' She pushed through the crowds; she stretched her hand and touched the clothes of Jesus. Her 12-year bleeding stopped! Jesus turned around and asked, 'Who touched my clothes?'

The woman told Jesus about her 12-year-long search for healing, her experiences with the various physicians and how she came to lose all her money without getting healed. And as Jesus listened, time passed. And just when Jesus said to her, 'Daughter, your faith has made you well, go in peace,' messengers from Jairus' house came with an announcement: 'The girl is dead. Don't bother to come.' In response, Jesus said to Jairus: 'Do not fear, only believe.' And they continued their journey to the house of Jairus.

Upon arrival, they found crowds mourning, and Jesus said to them: 'Why do you make a commotion and weep? The child is not dead, but sleeping.' The people laughed. But Jesus took the parents of the child and his three disciples, Peter, James and John, to the place where the 12-year-old child was. He took her hand and said to her '*talitha cum*', which means: 'little girl, get up'. And immediately she got up and began to walk about.

This story echoes many of the experiences of those suffering from HIV: patients who have been sick for a long time, patients who have spent all they had searching for healing, sick and dying young people, desperate parents trying to find healing for their children, those who weep for their dead children, women who sit at home, silently watching over their sick children, waiting for help to come.

But perhaps what is important is the difference – the difference that Jesus brings. Touching Jesus brings healing. He stops and wants to listen to the person who touched him rather than slip away from the risk of being deemed unclean. He brings hope where there is hopelessness. The bleeding woman who has searched for 12 years without any healing is suddenly healed and restored to the community as a daughter. Hope is restored as Jesus says to a fearful parent: 'Do not fear, only believe.' Indeed, hope is restored when Jesus makes those who mourn laugh.

The challenge for us is: how can Christians pronounce hope and life in the midst of despair and death? What clues does the story give us? Who can we identify with in the story?

There is Jairus who is a synagogue leader and Jesus, a celebrated teacher, healer and prophet. Then there are disciples, and three of these are identified as Peter, James and John. Apart from the crowds, there are three women: the bleeding woman, the sick and dying daughter of Jairus and the mother of this girl. None of the women is named and the bleeding woman is given neither name nor profession. Jairus, however, is given both. Both the woman and Jairus need the help of Jesus desperately. But their methods of approaching Jesus highlight their gendered identities. Jairus comes straight to Jesus and falls in front of him, saying: 'Come, lay your hands on my daughter so that she may be made well and live.' The bleeding woman, on the other hand, comes from behind Jesus. She does not speak and ask him. Instead, she decides that if she secretly touches the clothes of Jesus, she will be healed. Clearly the woman lacks words – rather in a typical gendered manner she speaks in action. It is only after Jesus had searched for her that she comes forward and makes a confession.

In fact, her behind-the-scenes approach highlights other gender stories of her life. Her illness was not only physical, but also one that gave her social stigma. Her illness would have meant that she was not allowed in certain places and possibly she could not marry. Turning to the other two women, the sick girl has no name of her own. She is identified through her father and her illness. We note also that she does not speak at all. Similarly, her mother is identified through her motherhood role, but she holds no public profession nor does she possess a name of her own. Like the other two women, she does not speak.

Despite these gender disparities, what are the models of gender empowerment offered to us by the story? Does the story offer us any model of women and men in partnership? There seem to be three models.

First, we are confronted by a *model of abuse of power,* embodied by the physicians. One can only suspect that over the years the woman's vulnerability and desperation has been exploited.

Second, we encounter a *model of using one's power to empower others.* Jairus and Jesus embody this model. Jairus, a synagogue leader, could have sent his servants to go and call Jesus, but rather he chooses to go there in person. Upon arrival, we note, he puts away whatever social status he may hold. He falls down and begs Jesus repeatedly, saying: 'My little daughter is at the point of death. Come and lay hands on her, so that she may be made well and live.' Jairus invites Jesus to use his power, to empower a powerless young girl.

In all these stages, Jesus insists on life and hope, knowing very well that a dead body would defile him. But he fights for the life of this young girl. He takes her hand and calls her back to life with '*talitha cum*'.

The third model offered by the story is that of *the oppressed becoming agents of their own empowerment*. This approach is best captured by the bleeding woman's search for healing. She pushes against the religious beliefs that hinder her from touching Jesus. She pushes against the crowds that also hinder her from reaching Jesus. She touches the clothes of Jesus and she gets healed. She becomes an agent of her own empowerment.

Yet even where the oppressed take control of their lives, it demands the willingness of the powerful to relinquish power. The powerful must be willing to feel power going out of them and accept it. They must share power with the powerless. It is not an easy thing. And hence the response of Jesus to a woman who sought to empower herself is important. It was only after meeting her and listening to her whole story that Jesus said to her: 'Daughter, your faith has made you well. Go in peace, and be healed of your disease.'

Reflection on the story invites a question: 'Who are you in the story?' Are you the powerful physicians who used their power to exploit and worsen the position of the powerless? Are you the powerful Jesus and Jairus, who are nonetheless willing to use their power to empower the powerless? Or, are you the bleeding woman, who is socially stigmatized, but who is willing to break the cultural and physical barriers to get her own healing?

THE WITNESS OF WOMEN

This litany invites reflection on women in the Bible and how women see themselves and are seen by others today. It uses 30 voices, but can be read by a smaller group, where each person reads more than one part. It should be read slowly and deliberately, with each woman lighting a candle after she has said her piece.

Litany

Woman 1   I am Eve, the bone of your bone, and the flesh of your flesh.

Woman 2   I am Sarah, the woman who calls you Lord and master.

Woman 3   I am Hagar, your maidservant; your unofficial wife.

Woman 4   I am Leah, the woman you married against your will.

Woman 5	I am Dinah, your only daughter who was raped.
Woman 6	I am Tamar, your desperate widow who played the sex worker.
Woman 7	I am Ruth, your widow sleeping at your feet, asking for your cover.
Woman 8	I am Bathsheba, seduced and married by your king.
Woman 9	I am Vashti, your wife, killed so that all women would obey their husbands.
Woman 10	I am the Levite's concubine, without a name, raped by the mob and cut to pieces by my lover.

All Women	We are the broken women of the Hebrew Bible.
	We are the broken women in a broken world.
	We are women searching for our own healing.

Woman 11	I am Mary, the pregnant woman with no place to go.
Woman 12	I am the Samaritan woman, with five husbands and none for her own.
Woman 13	I am Martha, the woman who is cooking while you sit and talk.
Woman 14	I am Mary, the woman who silently anoints your feet with oil.
Woman 15	I am the street woman, washing your feet with my tears.
Woman 16	I am the bent over woman, waiting for your healing touch.
Woman 17	I am the bleeding woman, struggling to touch your garment of power.
Woman 18	I am Anna, the widow praying for liberation.
Woman 19	I am the persistent widow in your courts, crying, 'Grant me justice.'
Woman 20	I am Jezebel, the demonized woman, blamed for all evil.

All Women	We are women of the New Testament.
	We are broken women in a broken world.
	We are women searching for our own healing.

Woman 21	I am the woman in your home; I am your wife.
Woman 22	I am the woman in your house; I am your lover, your live-in girlfriend.
Woman 23	I am the woman in your life; I am your mother.
Woman 24	I am a woman in the workplace; I am your secretary.

Woman 25	I am a woman in your streets; I am your sex worker.
Woman 26	I am a working woman in your house with no property of my own.
Woman 27	I am the woman in your life with no control over my body.
Woman 28	I am the woman in your bed with a blue eye and broken ribs.
Woman 29	I am the woman raped in your house, streets, offices and church.
Woman 30	I am the woman in your church, cooking, cleaning, clapping and dancing.
All Women	We are women of the world.
	And we are Christian women.
	We are broken women in a broken world
	We are women seeking for our own healing.

A GETHSEMANE MOMENT

Here are some facts and figures about the spread of HIV which high-light how gender inequality fuels the HIV epidemic worldwide. In the reflection that follows we are challenged to think about our own reaction to the spread of HIV, and to recognize our responsibility to 'stay awake and watch with me'.

Facts and figures

- ✠ Around half of all people living with HIV in the world are female.
- ✠ Globally, young women and girls are more susceptible to HIV than men and boys.
- ✠ Women are significantly more likely than men to experience HIV-related discrimination after infection.
- ✠ Women are dependent on male co-operation to protect them from infection.
- ✠ HIV has significantly increased the burden of care for family members for many women.
- ✠ In high prevalence countries, girls' enrolment at school has decreased in the past decade because girls are expected to care for sick relatives.

Reflection: Watch with me

Then Jesus went with his disciples to a place called Gethsemane, and he said to them, 'Sit here while I go over there and pray.' He took Peter and the two sons of Zebedee along with him, and he began to be sorrowful and troubled. Then he said to them, 'My soul is overwhelmed with sorrow to the point of death. Stay here and keep watch with me.'

Matthew 26.36–38

I suspect that for many of us the facts and figures of the HIV epidemic are daunting. Perhaps like Jesus in Gethsemane we will find our souls overwhelmed with sorrow.

How very much we would rather live in a world that HIV had never entered. And from heaven I hear God's compassion echoing that. How very much I long for that world too. We may groan like Jesus, 'Must we drink this cup?' But we must. That is the world in which we find ourselves. This is the Gethsemane the world must pass through.

Many are simply asleep, like the disciples a stone's throw from Jesus, simply unaware or unconcerned about the relentless threat in parts of the world far from them. And in streets very close to them.

Others come armed, as soldiers were preparing to do to Jesus. Armed with hatred; armed with prejudice; armed with selfish desire to distance themselves; armed with the potential to make money from the difficulty in which people find themselves.

And there are others who come as angels, as Luke tells us happened in Gethsemane, bringing strength to the one who had become weighed down with human frailty.

But even with ministers from God to strengthen and to comfort, this is a crisis that the world must endure. It is a cup we must drink. And just as crucifixion lay ahead for Jesus before he was raised to life, so there is a journey that the world must go – through death – before this epidemic is at an end.

Christians have a genuine role to play in being God's ministers in this Gethsemane. The lesson of Gethsemane is that God does not expect us to do what is impossible, but he does call us to be faithful in what we can do.

Transforming Lives – Stories of Change

This section outlines how lives have been transformed through the support and empowerment of Christian Aid partners, which has enabled people, often living in desperate circumstances, to find a foothold and turn their lives around. (You can find up-to-the-minute examples of Christian Aid's work at www.christianaid.org.uk.)

The stories illustrate the courage and resilience of many around the world who survive, despite the odds being stacked against them, and also the difference Christian Aid supporters can make both by their giving and campaigning.

The stories come from a variety of countries and describe different projects that Christian Aid supports, highlighting the areas of work its partner organizations are engaged in. As well as providing an aid for personal reflection, they can be used to illustrate the work Christian Aid is doing or to highlight issues in talks and sermons. With this in mind, suggestions are offered at the beginning of each story as to how it might fit with a liturgical theme.

REHABILITATION OF DISPLACED PEOPLE

Wherever there is war and conflict and lives are disrupted, it is usually poor people who suffer most because they have fewer resources to fall back on, either financial or educational, which would aid their rehabilitation. Christian Aid supports a number of partner organizations that work with displaced people trying to rebuild their lives in a post-conflict situation.

Seeds of hope – Angola

This story could be used at Advent to illustrate the coming of God's kingdom when swords are turned into ploughshares, or at Creation/Harvest time to symbolize the growth of new life.

José (pronounced Ho-zay) Batista Umba is the chief of a village called Kalunga Lunga in Angola. During the war in Angola in the late 1990s, he and the villagers were forced to flee the village for the anonymity of a large town when the soldiers encroached. Returning after the war, the villagers discovered that their village had all but been destroyed and that there was nothing to eat. They survived by eating whatever was growing wild. Help came in the form of an organization called ACM, the Angolan branch of the Young Man's Christian Association, which is funded by Christian Aid.

ACM gave José and the villagers seeds and tools to start farming again. Initially the villagers were so hungry that they ate some of the seeds instead of planting them. The ones they planted, however, grew and were harvested by the villagers; the first step in rebuilding their lives and community.

Involving the young – Sierre Leone

This story could be used around Remembrance Sunday to illustrate the rebuilding of lives after war and the importance of reconciliation.

Emmanuel Farma, 30, has had enough of conflict. When Sierre Leone erupted into civil war, his whole family fled their home in the eastern Kailahun district – one of the first areas to experience fighting. They reached comparative safety in the town of Kenema but two of the family died along the way. Emmanuel was to remain in Kenema because his family – like many others – never returned home after the war because their houses (and livelihoods) had been destroyed.

So when the Network Movement for Justice Development (NMJD) – a partner organization that Christian Aid linked up with after the war finished in 2002 – started to bring together youth groups to champion post-war development, Emmanuel knew he had to get involved. For NJMD, involving young people in its projects – from HIV education to ensuring the country's mines benefit the whole community – is essential to the rebuilding of Sierre Leone.

In 2003, Emmanuel was elected chair of the Kenema Coalition of Youth Groups; and he has used this role ever since to campaign for the inclusion of young Sierre Leoneans in decision-making so they can contribute positively to their local communities. He is passionate about improving living standards in Sierre Leone – eight years on after the war most Sierre Leoneans continue to live in grinding poverty – and believes the only way to do this is to put aside conflicts and work together.

It has not been easy in a country where youth have traditionally been left out of decision-making and discriminated against in favour of older people. But Emmanuel and NMJD are already achieving some success in the Kenema region. Youth in Simbaru and Tongo are finding work after taking up training opportunities provided through NMJD. And NMJD has helped young people improve their relationships with the community by getting them involved in projects such as the repairing of a local road between Joru and Mendekelema Gaura.

NMJD believes such initiatives are a necessity, not a luxury. Young people, who make up the majority of Sierre Leone's population, played a central part in the country's civil war, both as soldiers and civilians affected by the fighting. By addressing their challenges, NMJD believes it can help to bring lasting change for future generations of Sierre Leoneans.

Bringing families back together – The Democratic Republic of the Congo

This story might be used around Remembrance Day to illustrate the on-going tragedy of war, or at Christmas time when we celebrate the birth of Christ and think about the needs of children and family.

When Reverend Kambale Mangolopa set up a temporary home for 128 children displaced by fighting in the Democratic Republic of the Congo in 2008, he didn't know how long he would have to care for them or if they would ever be able to retrace their families. But by Decemeber – 12 months on from the crisis – the last of the chidren were reunited with their families.

The children were displaced by an escalation in violence of a 15-year conflict in which more than six million people have lost their lives. In 2008 it forced hundreds of thousands of people to flee their homes. Many children were at school or at home while their parents were working in the fields.

'Everyone had to run to safety as best as they could,' explains Reverend Kambale. 'Some of the children lost their parents along the way and were left to fend for themselves. They found their way home – it was like a word of mouth recommendation.'

Reverend Kambale's organization *Communauté Baptiste au centre de l'Afrique* (CBCA) set up the Unaccompanied Children's Centre by a church in Goma to care for the influx of children. The centre was a simple set of rooms around a courtyard where a small team of displaced mothers and women, some of whom had lost their own children, cared for them as volunteers. Christian Aid provided a grant from its emergency appeal to provide food, school fees and most crucially, support to help reunite them with their families.

Through their church networks, the Red Cross and UNICEF, CBCA passed the details and photos of the children through the refugee camps to retrace their relatives.

Gradually over the last year the children have returned to their villages to either their parents, or their nearest surviving relatives. Just before Christmas, the last five children returned home.

'For us it is an unexpected surprise that in an emergency like this CBCA has been able to reunite all of the children with their families,' says Jacques Miaglia, Christian Aid's Country Manager. 'It makes it all worth it.'

Educating for peace – Angola

This story could be used around Remembrance Day to illustrate the desire for peace on the part of those who endure conflict. As it symbolizes new life, it also resonates with the Easter narrative.

An elastic band is the entire toy collection of 13-year-old Eduardo Palanga. Outside his home in Angola he plays a game called *pisto*. To play it, you flick an elastic band against a wall so that it bounces off and lands on the ground. Your friend then flicks his or her elastic band in the same way and, if it lands on yours, gets to keep it. Eduardo only has one elastic band left.

When the soldiers came to Eduardo's village during the war, his family ran away to the mountains. They survived there for a week. When they came back, they discovered that buildings in the village had been ruined during the fighting. Eduardo's classroom had no roof, desks or chairs. 'When it rained all the water came in,' explains Eduardo. 'We didn't have chairs, so we sat on stones.'

Using money given by Christian Aid supporters, ACM (Angola's branch of the Young Men's Christian Association) has helped the community to rebuild the roof, put shutters on the windows and supplied desks with seats. 'I like school now. I have got eight exercise books, two pens, a pencil and a rubber. But, I don't have a ruler or coloured pencils yet,' says Eduardo.

He continues: 'I don't know why there was a war. I want to have peace, not war. Now there is peace, I feel safer at home, knowing that we won't have to run away again.'

To build and to plant – Angola

This story could be used at Harvest time to illustrate the theme of plant-
ing and reaping or at Eastertide when thinking about fresh starts and
new beginnings. If your church community celebrates Education Sun-
day, this story carries within it the importance of education.

Twelve-year-old Servina Marta lives with her family in their village
called Kiola, in Kwanza Sul province in western Angola. But in 1992,
before Servina was born, her parents had to leave the village which
was under threat of attack by UNITA's army. They moved to Wako-
Kungo, the nearest town, for safety. There they made a meagre living
selling firewood. In June 2002, it was safe to return to Kiola and the
family moved back. Servina's parents went first, leaving their six children in Wako-Kungo. When they had built a house, they sent for their
children.

At first the family had a little food from the city, but they did not
have tools or seeds to start to grow food for themselves. Servina had to
make the long journey into the town nearly every day to sell firewood
to make some money for the family. 'I had to leave home at about eight
o'clock, and I got to Wako-Kungo at about one o'clock. I carried the
firewood on my head. It was very heavy,' she explains.

But Christian Aid's partner, ACM (Angola's branch of the Young
Man's Christian Association) helped the family to rebuild their farm
again. ACM gave the family maize and beans to plant, and lentils to
eat, until the crops grew. Gradually, the family were able to start a
new, peaceful life in Kiola. This help meant that Servina did not have
to travel to the city to sell firewood so often. After the first harvest, the
family had enough maize to eat, and saved some seed to plant the next
year. ACM also gave them seed potatoes for the following year, and
has given the community oxen to make ploughing easier.

When the Kiola community returned after the end of the civil war,
the first thing they did was to rebuild the school so that the children
could catch up on their disrupted education. Now Servina does not
have to go to the city so often to sell firewood, she is able to go to
school every afternoon. 'I only go [into the city] if I need to buy something like an exercise book for school,' she says. Her favourite subject
is maths, and she would like to be a teacher when she is older: 'I help
with the children at home and I like teaching them.'

Servina's mother, Domingas Noguera, described the difference that
ACM's help has made: 'There was a lot of suffering when we first

arrived. Now we are taking our first steps to make things better . . . If ACM hadn't come to help us, we'd be dead.'

PROMOTING HEALTHCARE

Defending healthcare – Israel and the Occupied Palestinian Territory

This story could be used around Remembrance Day to emphasize the importance of reconciliation where there is conflict, or at Christmas time when thinking about the need for peace, particularly in the Holy Land.

Physicians for Human Rights-Israel (PHR-I) was set up to defend healthcare as a basic right in Israel and the Occupied Palestinian Territory, where there is on-going conflict. Every weekend, Israeli doctors and nurses volunteer their time to PHR-I and, alongside the Palestinian Medical Relief Society, run mobile clinics offering basic medical care and treatment to villagers in parts of the West Bank with reduced access to healthcare due to the military occupation of their lands.

One such volunteer is Ilana Rathouse, an Israeli nurse from Tel Aviv who speaks Arabic and is a human rights activist. She says of her work at the clinic: 'I assess people's needs and take the blood pressure of patients. I also assist the doctor. Last time we had a clinic we had to carry out six minor operations.' But for her, the real value is in creating a non-military encounter between Israelis and Palestinians. 'It is as though we are creating the threads of an embroidery upon which peace can be built.'

Labouring for new life – Angola

This story could be used to illustrate post-conflict rebuilding in a Remembrance Day context, or at Advent and Christmas time when we think of the birth of the Christ child. It might even be used to think about the importance of motherhood on Mothering Sunday.

Evalina Wandi Prata has excellent medical skills. She has worked for much of her life as a midwife. However, like so many others, during the war in the late 1990s, she was forced to flee. Having gone on the run three times, she lost many of her possessions, including the papers that showed she was qualified as a midwife.

But now that the war is over she has been able to gain her qualifications all over again, thanks to a centre run by a Christian Aid partner organization called IECA, the Angolan Congregational Church. 'We will save many lives,' Evalina says. 'I decided to become a midwife because I wanted to prevent babies from dying. Too many babies die in Angola . . . I am going to have a good future now, because I have a profession.' She wants her children to have the chance to learn and never to have to endure war again. 'I think and I hope that the babies I deliver will live in a better world.'

Pre- and post-natal care – Burkina Faso

Because many women in Burkina Faso do not have access to a health centre to give birth, it's extremely important that traditional birth attendants understand basic midwifery skills and hygiene. Christian Aid's partner ODE, *Office de Développement des Eglises Evangéliques* – the development wing of the Evangelical Churches of Burkina Faso, trains attendants in pre- and post-natal care as well as HIV awareness and how to prevent transmission of the virus from mother to child.

Life-saving skills – Angola

This story could be used on Mothering Sunday or Education Sunday.

Tabita Benir de Jesus lives in Angola and has trained as a cook at a centre run by Christian Aid partner, IECA, the Angolan Congregational Church. The skills she has learnt there have been lifesavers in more ways than one. Before she took courses in cookery, health education and human rights, she scraped a living by crossing the border into a neighbouring country, buying clothes and bringing them back to her home to sell. It meant that she had to leave her young children, Josue and Jaeli (prounounced Joz-way and Ji-ye-lee) for half of every month. But now, thanks to IECA and her determination to learn, Tabitha works at home baking cakes and catering for parties. The money she now earns is enough to pay for the children to go to school.

Her new skills saved the children's lives recently. They both developed malaria, but because Tabitha had taken a health education course, she recognized the symptoms immediately and knew exactly what was needed to make them better. 'I am happy now,' says Tabitha. 'This centre is a way of education and informing women in Angola. It needs to continue. Its work is very welcome because it frees women from just doing domestic tasks.'

EDUCATION

A brighter future – Bangladesh

This story could be used on Education Sunday, at Eastertide to illustrate transformation and new beginnings.

During the past decade, Bangladesh has made significant progress towards fulfilling children's rights to an education with 82 per cent boys and 86 per cent girls enrolling in primary schools. However, these improvements do not equate to *all* children. There are still more than three million children out of school with access particularly difficult for *adivasi* children (children of indigenous tribes) and those living in remote rural areas. Christian Aid partner the Christian Commission for Development in Bangladesh (CCDB) runs 240 pre-school centres that help children prepare for entry to formal primary schools.

In the communities where CCDB works, the majority of people are illiterate or semi-illiterate. CCDB recognizes that it is important to motivate the parents and help them understand the important role that education plays in their children's future. Last year, CCDB helped 7,640 children at its 240 pre-school centres and the organization has helped 991 children to enrol in primary schools.

Shurabhi Mardi is 10 years old and a former classmate at one of CCDB's pre-school centres. Her mother Rani Hasda is member of the Amia Kathal Adivasi Surjadai forum. Shurabhi's father is paralysed and her 15-year-old brother is unemployed, so the family is entirely dependent on Rani and whatever she can earn as a day labourer.

Through her involvement in a woman's group run by CCDB, Rani decided to send Shurabhi to the pre-school centre. Shurabhi flourished and is now studying at a primary school. She continues to thrive and even came top in her class last year.

Shurabhi is committed to her studies and wants to continue her education so that she 'can bring a smile to my parents' face'.

INCOME GENERATION

Breeding pigs – The Democratic Republic of Congo

This story could be used on Mothering Sunday to illustrate the wider concept of 'mothering' or at harvest to highlight growth from small beginnings.

Madame Ntalani's grandchildren were orphaned when their parents died of an HIV-related illness. HIV is a virus that has robbed millions of children of their parents, and many elderly people have found themselves bringing up young families at a stage of life when they themselves should be receiving extra help. Wonderfully, Madame Ntalani took eight children into her home, despite having no source of income to keep them. It was an act of great goodness, but the family faced desperate poverty.

AMO-Congo, an organization supported by Christian Aid, helped the family. It gave them two pigs, which have produced piglets. By selling the piglets, Madame Ntalani has been able to help feed her grandchildren. Nadia, the eldest, has been able to start school with her fees paid by AMO-Congo, giving her hope for a better future.

Breeding goats – Bolivia

This story illustrates the theme of growth and would be ideal for harvest time.

Christian Aid partner Causananchispaj (pronounced Cow-san-an-chis-pak) helped set up a cooperative in Huichaca, an isolated village in Bolivia. It provided the community with a 'rotating fund' of livestock. This gives people the chance to 'borrow' 'white goats', which have a higher milk yield than other breeds. After the goats breed, the kids can be returned to the fund and benefit even more people.

Weaving carpets – Afghanistan

This story could be used in several ways – during Advent when the stories of Elizabeth and Mary help us to focus on the lives of women and their relationships, at harvest time, when we think about seeds or growth, or during Lent when we assess our own lifestyles and our priorities.

Afghanistan is the poorest country in the world outside Africa, with less than a third of the population having access to clean water. Forty per cent do not meet their daily food needs. More than half the population live below the poverty line. Christian Aid works at a structural level in Afghanistan, lobbying for the implementation of human rights – especially women's rights – at the social and political level. But when people are wondering where the next meal will come from, when they only ate bread yesterday and may not eat today, income generation is a critical activity.

Tajvar Vozmarha, aged 40, is desperately poor. Her husband is too old to do any heavy work and they have almost no income. Christian Aid partner CRDSA is teaching Tajvar to weave traditional Afghan carpets to supplement her family's income. At the time of writing, she is working on her first rug. It will take her three months or more to make, but she hopes to sell it for about $100. This profit will be enough to feed her family for a month.

Flowing milk – Haiti

This provides a good harvest story, helping to illustrate growth from humble beginnings, and of our need to work together to produce a 'harvest'.

Some Haitian milk used to flow straight down the drain. Unable to compete with powdered and condensed milk imported from Europe and North America, small-scale Haitian farmers could not make a living, and poured milk away in frustration. Milk was being wasted as farmers could not reach consumers effectively, but a Christian Aid supported dairy project '*Lat Agogo*' (Milk Flows) has helped them reach the market. Now flowing milk means farmers are looking to a better future with a regular income for their families.

Christian Aid partner organization Veterimed helps farmers to set up and run the dairies. It provides training and advice to farmers, and veterinary care for their livestock. Milk is sterilized or turned into yoghurt and advertised with a catchy song on local radio. The products are delivered to shops and restaurants in the city – markets that a small farmer working on his own couldn't afford to access. Profits from the diary are returned to the farmers at the end of the year in the form of a pump or a water tank – something the whole community can use.

Recycling wood – Hondurus

This project illustrates well the idea of sustainable development and would be ideal to use in a creation centered service.

COPRODEDPIY (Yaramaringüila Committee for Indigenous Rights and Development) works in central Honduras, where deforestation has caused environmental problems and made it difficult to grow crops. It has helped set up a sustainable carpentry project that uses only recycled or sustainable wood. The money from selling the wooden products enables the carpenter to stay in his community, rather than having to look for work in the city.

CONSERVATION FARMING

Replenishing the soil – Zimbabwe

This story could be used in several ways – to illustrate a harvest or creation theme, or on Mothering Sunday as it tells of the ingenuity of Daisy, mother to seven children.

The situation in Zimbabwe is extremely difficult. One in ten children will die before their fifth birthday. At the time of writing, 80 per cent of Zimbabweans are registered as unemployed. Drought, ruined infrastructure and an economy in collapse mean people simply can't grow enough food to survive. The 'hunger' season, when food runs out, can leave as many as five million people dependent on food aid.

Christian Aid's network of partner organizations on the ground means that we can reach thousands of poor families. Daisy Moyo is 48 and has benefited enormously from the approach pioneered by Christian Aid partner ZimPro. She cares for seven children, including one grandchild. Daisy grows maize, groundnuts, sorghum and cowpeas. ZimPro has showed her how to make the best use of water and the natural resources available to her in the drought-prone area where she lives. For Daisy's oldest daughter, Sithandekile, who is living with HIV, having enough to eat, and a variety of food available, is extremely important if she is to stay well. The family now has almost three times as much food to eat and sell, and has escaped extreme poverty.

With enough food, families such as Daisy's will be better able to survive the hunger, HIV and other diseases that needlessly claim lives in Zimbabwe.

A new agriculture – India

This is a good harvest story, as well as providing possibilities for Easter and Pentecost.

Chandramma Moligeri was born a 'weeder'. As a dalit woman, she worked for most of her life in others' fields, in exchange for grain or small amounts of money. Struggling to feed her family and with little chance or escaping the legacy of the Indian caste system, she lived unnoticed on the margins of society.

Chanramma's life was turned around when she joined a local women's group, or *sangham*, supported by Christian Aid partner the Deccan Development Society (DDS). These women cleared an area of drought-prone wasteland and farmed it, using traditional methods learned from DDS. Slowly, they restored life to their land – and then brought the celebration of an enormous harvest to their whole community.

In sanghams across the Medak district of Andhra Pradesh, DDS now works with 5,000 women. These women have decided to do something amazing. From their excess harvest, they have helped to feed 50,000 of the poorest people in their communities.

And the women are now passing on their knowledge. DDS is training them to use film and radio to raise awareness and campaign on issues such as climate change. Now their skills and passion are helping communities throughout Andhra Pradesh to share in the joy of harvest.

As for Chandramma, she is no longer reliant on others for handouts. Instead, she has become a landowner herself. 'I am the only person I know who has passed on land to her daughters,' she tells us with a twinkle in her eye.

NATURAL DISASTER

Floods – India

This story highlights problems associated with climate change and could be used in a creation-centered service.

In October 2009, devastating floods struck the southern Indian states of Andhra Pradesh and Karnataka, affecting millions of people. And in August 2008, poorly maintained infrastructure led to flooding on a dramatic scale in the north Indian state of Bihar.

Climate change is likely to make extreme weather events like this more frequent and severe. Poor infrastructure, poverty and vulnerability intensify the effects of climate-related disasters.

In 2009, Christian Aid initiated a groundbreaking climate-change education campaign with its partner SEEDS. This was aimed at children in 10,000 schools across five states in India, and provided activities on helping communities adapt to the impact of the changing climate.

Acknowledgements and Sources

The editor and publisher gratefully acknowledge permission to use copyright material. Every effort has been made to trace sources of material, but any omissions will be rectified in future printings.

Part One Seasonal Liturgies

Advent
Looking Backwards and Forwards © Diakonia Council of Churches, South Africa
Preparing the Way of the Lord: Juggling Our Priorities © Christian Aid
  with extracts from Lewis Carroll, *Alice Through the Looking Glass*; D. H. Lawrence, 'Pax'.
From Darkness to Light: A Service for World AIDS's Day © South African Council of Churches

Christmas
The Gift of Life © Christian Aid
  with extract from Janet Morley

Epiphany
Journeys © Christian Aid
  with extract from Walt Whitman, 'Pioneers, O pioneers!'

Lent
Making Choices © Christian Aid
  with extract from PACSA (Pietermaritzburg Agency for Christian Social Awareness), South Africa
A short service of repentance, reconciliation and healing © South African Council of Churches
  with extract from The Iona Community

Holy Week

Palm Sunday
Finding our voices: no to violent crime © South African Council of Churches
  with extract from an adapted Palestinian litany by Munib A. Youman

Maundy Thursday
The kiss © Christian Aid
  with extract from Bonaventura

Good Friday
Through the cross © Diakonia Council of Churches, South Africa
How long? © Christian Aid

Easter
All things are made new: a short service of renewal © South Africa Council of
  Churches
From slavery to freedom © Christian Aid

Pentecost
Come, Holy Spirit © Christian Aid
In the power of the Spirit © South African HIV/AIDS consultative process
Lock in © Christian Aid

Creation and harvest
A service of thanksgiving © Methodist Church of South Africa
Taking time . . . © Christian Aid
  with extract from Walt Whitman, 'Pioneers, O pioneers!'
Celebrating creation © Christian Aid
  with extract from Mary Oliver, 'The Summer Day'; Kate McIlhagga, 'The
  green heart of the snowdrop'; Wild Goose Worship Group, *A wee worship
  book*; Andrew de Smet and Chris Polhill.
Not carbon neutral © Christian Aid
Boys and girls come out to pray © Christian Aid
  with extract from Maya Angelou, 'Pretty woman'; William Shakespeare, *Hamlet*; Julian of Norwich, *Revelations of divine love*

The season of remembrance
Offering an olive branch © Christian Aid
Rites of reconciliation © South African Council of Churches
Love one another: an Agape meal (adapted) © PACSA (Pietermaritzburg Agency
  for Christian Social Awareness), South Africa
  with extract from College of Transfigurations HIV/AIDS service 'Being Lifted
  up', Grahamstown; Jan Berry, Sheffield, from Janet Morley, *All Desires
  Known*; Jim Cotter, 'Eternal Spirit, life-giver'; World Conference for Reli-
  gion and Peace; World Council of Churches, *Africa Praying: World Council
  of Churches Resources for Sermons and Liturgy*; Diocese of Natal's Women's
  Conference, 'Ekuphelelisweni /Moving to wholeness'; PACSA, *Agape Service
  Book*.

Everyday services
An order for Morning Prayer © The Methodist Church, South Africa
An order for Evening Prayer © The Methodist Church, South Africa
A children's service © The Methodist Church, South Africa

Part Two Prayers

Opening prayers

We come together to declare the goodness of God © Christian Aid
Come, Lord, share this time with us © Ecumenical Advocacy Alliance
Holy God, you created one humanity © Christian Aid
Creator God © Christian Aid
God calls us together © Christian Aid
The earth belongs to God, the earth and all its people © Christian Aid
Let all that is visible, worship the Lord © Christian Aid
Our help is in the name of the eternal God © South African Council of
  Churches
For all who reach out to God © South African Council of Churches

Confession and absolution

Loving God, you make us in your image (adapted) © Christian Aid
All knowing God © South African Council of Churches
Merciful God, we confess © Christian Aid
Eternal God, we confess to you our sinfulness, Sri Lanka
Lord God, we repent of our denial and complacency © Diakonia Council of
  Churches, South Africa
Merciful God, you keep your promise of forgiveness (adapted) © Ecumenical
  Advocacy Alliance
Jesus, Son of God, Son of man and woman © PACSA (Pietermaritzburg Agency
  for Christian Social Awareness), South Africa
Merciful God, we meet each other today at this cross (adapted) © Robin Green
O God, whose longing is to reconcile the whole universe within your love ©
  PACSA (Pietermaritzburg Agency for Christian Social Awareness), South
  Africa
God of peace, forgive us (adapted) © Christian Aid
O God, in whose body was named © PACSA (Pietermaritzburg Agency for Chris-
  tian Social Awareness), South Africa
Search me, O God © The Methodist Church, South Africa
O Christ, for whom we search © Janet Morley
God of healing © Christian Aid

Prayers and collects

May none of God's wonderful works keep silence, 3rd Century North African
  monastic community
Spirit of life in the dust and the sunshine © Christian Aid
We stand side-by-side © Christian Aid
Underneath me are two feet © Christian Aid
O God, you have prepared in peace, Traditional Ethiopian
Grant, O God, your protection © The Methodist Church, South Africa
Almighty God, our heavenly Father, the privilege is ours © Church of the Prov-
  ince, West Indies
God of abundance © Christian Aid
Generous God © Christian Aid

Gracious Lord, we give you our will © Christian Aid
Like a mother (Woman of Ethiopia) © Annabel Shilson-Thomas
Subversive God (adapted) © Christian Aid
Love incarnate © Christian Aid
As I enter the street market © Christian Aid
Gracious Father © Christian Aid
Creator God © Christian Aid
Lord, you placed us in the world © Christian Aid
Kumba Yah, my Lord ('Someone's crying Lord') © Asian women doing theology,
    Hong Kong
We pray for all woman and children © Diakonia Council of Churches, South
    Africa
Dear God © Diakonia Council of Churches, South Africa
Holy God © Diakonia Council of Churches, South Africa
God of all the world (adapted) © Christian Aid
Compassionate God (adapted) © Christian Aid
Hear me, Jesus © Christian Aid
Praise our God, O peoples, from Psalm 66: 8–20

Prayers of commitment
God of power © Diakonia Council of Churches, South Africa
God of the impossible (adapted) © Christian Aid
After the rain © Peter Graystone, Christian Aid
As I drink my coffee © Christian Aid
God of infinite wisdom and grace © Diakonia Council of Churches, South
    Africa
We believe that beyond violence © PACSA (Pietermaritzburg Agency for Chris-
    tian Social Awareness), South Africa
Lord God, give us the spirit of courage © Diakonia Council of Churches, South
    Africa
We reject all forms of discrimination © Diakonia Council of Churches, South
    Africa

Intercessions
In gratitude to God © Diakonia Council of Churches, South Africa
We pray for poor people © Christian Aid
God our Father © Diakonia Council of Churches, South Africa
For children who suffer pain and degradation © PACSA (Pietermaritzburg
    Agency for Christian Social Awareness), South Africa
Our God, heal us from social structures (adapted) © South African Council of
    Churches
We are all affected by HIV © Diakonia Council of Churches, South Africa
Loving God © Diakonia Council of Churches, South Africa

Blessings
The blessings of our gracious God © Christian Aid
May God the Father bless us © Christian Aid
May the God of the poor © Diakonia Council of Churches, South Africa

May Christ who healed the bent-over woman, source unknown
May God our loving parent © Diakonia Council of Churches
May the blessing of the God of peace and justice © South African Council of Churches
Go out into the world © Diakonia Council of Churches
Lord bless us © Christian Aid
May the Lord watch over you, Celtic blessing
A blessing on the men and on the women © Christian Aid
In our living and our loving © Christian Aid

Sending out
Loving God (adapted) © Christian Aid
Walk with those who stumble, source unknown, adaptation by Annabel Shilson-Thomas

Part Three Biblical Reflections

Being one body © Diakonia Council of Churches, South Africa
Stewardship of creation © Christian Aid
Sharing our harvest © Christian Aid
God's bias © Christian Aid
Hearing the Bible through other people's eyes © Christian Aid
Gender and power (adapted) © Diakonia Council of Churches, South Africa
The witness of women © Diakonia Council of Churches, South Africa
A Gethsemane moment © Christian Aid

Part Three Transforming Lives – Stories of Change

All © Christian Aid